The Remarkable

(Women's Suffrage)

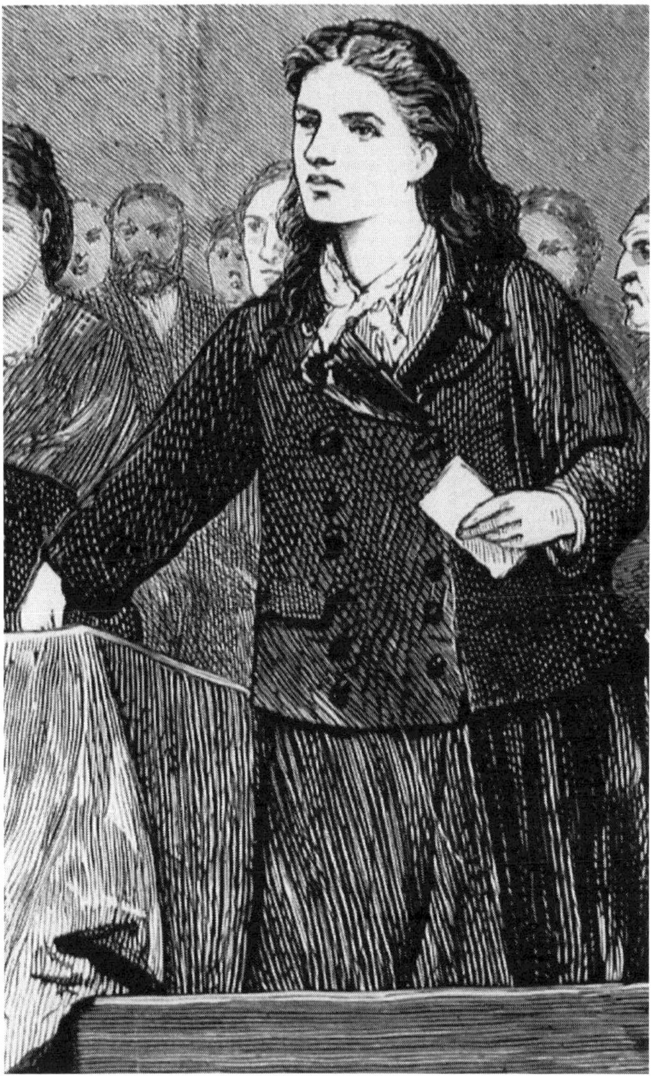

By

Graeme Taylor

The Remarkable Rhoda Garrett (Women's Suffrage)

by

Graeme Taylor

ISBN: 978-0-9933555-3-0

This book is published by Graeme Taylor in conjunction with **WRITERSWORLD**, and is produced entirely in the UK. It is available to order from most bookshops in the United Kingdom, and is also globally available via UK based Internet book retailers.

Copy Edited by Ian Large

Cover Design by Jag Lall

WRITERSWORLD
2 Bear Close Flats, Bear Close, Woodstock
Oxfordshire, OX20 1JX, England
☎ 01993 812500
☎ +44 1993 812500

www.writersworld.co.uk

The text pages of this book are produced via an independent certification process that ensures the trees from which the paper is produced come from well managed sources that exclude the risk of using illegally logged timber while leaving options to use post-consumer recycled paper as well.

Contents

List of Illustrations

Introduction

So why write a book on Rhoda Garrett? Who was she? Why is she not a household name? How come she has two pieces of music dedicated to her? Was she that remarkable?

In this book, I will endeavour to answer the above questions and hopefully you, the reader, will agree with me that Rhoda Garrett was a most remarkable person.

I will answer the first one straightaway. A few years ago, I was helping my Mum (Mary Taylor BEM) research and write a book entitled *Winds of Change in a Sleepy Sussex Village – Rustington* and whilst researching this book I came across the names of two former residents of the village, namely Rhoda Garrett and her cousin Agnes Garrett. I started to delve deeper into Rhoda's past and was becoming more and more fascinated by her life story.

Further questions were starting to spring up for me, such as:

Why did Rhoda express her wish to be buried in the churchyard of St Peter and St Paul, Rustington, West Sussex when she died at 2 Gower Street, London?

Why doesn't her gravestone still exist?

How did she know one of the other famous Rustington residents Sir Hubert Parry and his aristocratic wife Lady Maud(e) Parry (nee Herbert)? (Her birth certificate says Maud but she tended to use Maude.)

After much research, I have found out answers to most of the above questions but as to why her gravestone does not still exist, I have not been able to deduce the reason. I can only give my thoughts in the book and leave the reader to decide for themselves.

As part of my research, Mum and I went to see the late Laura Ponsonby and her sister Kate, direct descendants of Sir Hubert and Lady Maude Parry, at Shulbrede Priory to look at the diaries of the great composer, his wife and their daughter Dolly (Dorothea). Laura immediately picked up my interest in Rhoda and showed me a couple of rare letters written by her and, moreover, a tribute to Rhoda Garrett written by Lady Maude, which she told me that no one outside the family had ever seen before.

I can think of no better way to introduce Rhoda Garrett to you than to include, in full, this fantastic tribute, which includes an amazing pen and ink sketch of Rhoda drawn by Lady Maude along with the illuminated "R" in her name.

PEN-AND-INK SKETCHES.

RHODA GARRETT.

RHODA GARRETT was born in 1841. She was the eldest daughter of the Rev. John F. Garrett, rector of Elton, in Derbyshire, and first cousin to Mrs. Garrett Anderson and to Mrs. Fawcett. She and an elder sister of Mrs. Fawcett's came up to London in search of employment in 1867. They succeeded, after many a weary and fruitless search, in apprenticing themselves to an architect for three years, lady pupils in an architect's office being a thing altogether undreamt and unheard of. Having learnt their trade, they soon established themselves as decorators in 2, Gower Street, their firm being the first and only one registered for ladies. A cottage room exhibited by them in the Trocadéro at the French Exhibition of 1878 gained very general admiration for its original and simple style; and the Miss Garretts, after long protracted and patient work attained that success which was so justly their due. A manual written by the cousins, addressed particularly to the middle classes, containing their views on house decoration, passed through six editions; and in it are illustrations of the interior of their house in Gower Street. They helped materially to assist in the revolution art has made during these last few years against vulgarity and show, in making homes more artistic and refined. By way of assisting themselves in their profession they spent a great deal of time travelling over England studying the interior fittings of old houses both in the country and in towns. Thus they imbibed as much as possible the spirit of the fine old works of art which have descended to us, and translated it into their own work. Their mantelpieces and wall-papers are especially characteristic, some of them being really beautiful. Indeed, they were among the foremost revivers of the so-called Queen Anne school—an indefinite period which no one takes strictly to mean between the years 1702 and 1714. It is said that Rhoda Garrett thought at one time of becoming an architect, and her powers no doubt would have been equal to the undertaking. Form especially attracted her. She loved to wander over old churches and buildings, examining ancient mouldings and carvings, and the noble proportions of architecture. It was no wonder that struggling artists found in her so ready and efficient a friend. If their work was really thorough and good, she would spare no pains or trouble to assist them to the best of her power.

Irrational opposition is certain to arise against people of any independence of mind or breadth of view, but Rhoda Garrett was not easily daunted. Nor from fear of being thought strong-minded or unfeminine did she hesitate to become an earnest supporter of woman's rights, for to the cause of justice she could not but lend a helping hand. Almost the last act of her life was to write a letter of sympathy to the promoters of the Scottish National Demonstration of Women, which had just been held in Glasgow. Numerous and varied were her interests. She was a member of the Royal Archæological Institute, and also belonged to the Society for the Protection of Ancient Buildings.

Delicate health at length obliged Rhoda Garrett to seek repose for at least a few months in the year; and her happiest days were spent in the country at Rustington, a village in Sussex, close by the sea. Here she took a cottage, and surrounded herself with congenial friends and pet animals, including dogs.

Early in the November of 1882 she was taken ill with typhoid fever, and her constitution, already worn out by incessant toil, was unable to resist the attack. She died on November 22nd, and was buried at Rustington, in the little churchyard where she had herself expressed a wish to rest.

In the world we rarely meet with a truly noble and ideal character. There are many whom we admire for various fine qualities, but a complete human being is a thing so rare that we may live our whole lives through without ever coming across anybody whose humanity impresses us in its very best and widest sense. The world, indeed, is slow to recognise such, and it is only when death has taken them, and we are left in darkness, no longer illumined by their bright and vivid presence, that we fully realise the immensity of our loss. Those who knew Rhoda Garrett felt, indeed, that she was one of those few and exceptional beings whose personality was strong enough to influence for good all those with whom she came in contact. She seemed to complete other natures, so that in losing her many have felt that they have lost the very best part of themselves. Framing a high standard of what her friends ought to be, her vivid imagination credited them with fine qualities, and the sense that she expected such things of them, made them, at least, strive not to disappoint her, even if they did not, in fact, attain to her ideal.

With such a standard, she would never

allow herself to be content with low aims or ideals, but strove always to elevate and dignify humdrum lives and common place surroundings. Eminently social, she gathered round her a large circle of friends. She used to say she loved every man, woman, and child; and, indeed, her tenderness and love for children was a strongly marked feature in her character.

To define genius is almost an impossibility, but there is one quality which is almost a certain test of it—the quality of humour. This quality Rhoda Garrett possessed to a degree almost unparalleled, and it was one of the traits which made her so lovable. Humour is invariably united with the deepest and tenderest feelings of our nature, and those who have it most are inevitably those who feel the most. It seems almost impossible to describe such a many-sided character. To see Rhoda Garrett was to feel her, and she left a deep mark wherever she went. One of her peculiar charms was her unexpectedness. Her moods were so various, and she was so totally unlike any one else, that it was always impossible to tell what she was going to say or do next. These kinds of surprises lent a certain excitement to her society. No subject ever came amiss to her, for she approached and discussed every question with large-minded liberality, and without conscious effort; and in her own home, surrounded as she was by beautiful and worthy objects of art, all seemed to breathe, whilst with her, a purer and a higher atmosphere.

Delicate, sensitive, and sympathetic, it would have been impossible for her to have lived and worked alone, but, fortunately, she found in her cousin, Agnes Garrett, one ready to sympathise and able to share in all her labours.

These two cousins attained very considerable eminence as house decorators, by which means they supported not only themselves, but young and otherwise helpless relations. It was in the face of no uncommon difficulties that Rhoda Garrett started her career in life, but by her earnest, steadfast use of more than ordinary abilities she vanquished and overcame and was successful. Above all other virtues she admired that of unselfishness, and unselfish she was not so much in the ordinary acceptation of the term, but in a broader and more general kind of way.

She showed it most in her never-ceasing thoughtfulness for her friends, and in her wide-spreading generosity. An almost divine power of forgiveness of injuries characterised her life throughout, and this was the more remarkable in one of so quick a temper and so excitable a disposition.

With her wide and generous sympathies for mankind in general, Rhoda Garrett could not be otherwise than a sincere Radical; and she more especially had at heart the cause of woman's suffrage, and the kindred subjects of woman's position and opportunities in the world. Those who heard her speak in public will never forget the impression of that beautiful voice, with its ring of truth and earnestness, carrying conviction as nothing else could; and yet, though burning with a genuine enthusiasm, her speeches were as remarkable for their reasonableness as for their eloquence. A few words from a speech of hers are worth quoting to show her justice and breadth of view on the subject of women's work:

"This question rests mainly in your own hands. Now the public recognises and, for the most part, it sympathises with your demand to earn your own living. But the public will not pay you for unmarketable commodities. It will not, because you are women, remove all difficulties out of your path. It will, indeed, often hinder you, and often sneer at you; but it cannot stop you, and it will generally deal fairly with you if you show that you know how to do thoroughly what you undertake to do. Let women, then, take advantage of the greater facilities of higher education which are placed within their reach. Let them learn to be thoroughly reasonable and earnest in all the work that they undertake—not blown about by every wind of doctrine, and running hither and thither after six things at a time; and then the time will come, I am convinced, when women, as well as men, will be free to choose their own careers—such careers, that is, as are found by experience fit and best for their capabilities and their natures. Ladies, this is my advice to women, and it is based upon experience."

The clearness of expression and well-balanced distribution of thought in this passage is sufficient to show that she had unusual readiness in appealing to an audience, and yet no one ever hated speaking more than she did. It was only her enthusiasm for the cause of women and her strong sense of duty that enabled her to pass through such an ordeal.

The true artist invests even the most simple and ordinary things with interest, and in Rhoda Garrett there was so much fulness and freshness of life that the beautiful appealed to her in almost every form. Music, poetry, and painting, flowers, and all things lovely, seemed to pass into her and become part of her very being; and, inasmuch as she always thought for herself, and was independent of conventional formulas, the work which resulted from her impressions was marked by the best kind of originality, free from either affectation or effort—the natural outcome of her feelings.

So much the poorer is the world for the loss of such an original being—yet Rhoda Garrett will not have lived in vain. The force of her example will tell upon the many who have known her, and inspire women especially to care and strive for good and noble objects, such as the happiness and welfare of the race. Her influence will tend greatly to diminish charlatanism, for with her honest and sincere nature she had a holy horror of shams of all sorts. Women are too often inclined to assume cleverness, and with no real basis for the assumption, they delude only the foolish, and thus bring their sex into disrepute. A simple unworldly life like Rhoda Garrett's, without pretension, will do more to make women respected than the thousands of overwrought and over-balanced creatures whose whole energies are expended in ill-considered chatter.

Our existence would be a dreary one if we were not occasionally cheered and invigorated by meeting with exceptional and uncommon people, who make us not only aspire after virtue but believe in its actual existence.

Thus are our days made sweeter to us, and our darkness penetrated by the light of true genius. When such beings die, they remain as shining examples to those who follow after; and, loved as Rhoda Garrett was in life, she will not be forgotten in death.

The words of the American poet seem applicable to her—

"Dear friend whoever you are, here take this kiss,
I give it especially to you—do not forget me,
I feel like one who has done his work—I progress on—
(Long enough have I dallied with Life,)
The unknown sphere more real than I dream'd, more direct, darts awakening rays about me—so long!
Remember my words—I love you—
I depart from materials,
I am as one disembodied, triumphant, dead."

MAUDE PARRY.

Chapter 1
Elton, Derbyshire

Rhoda Garrett was born on 28th March 1841 at Parsonage House in Well Street, Elton to the Reverend John Fisher Garrett and his wife Elizabeth Henzey Pidcock.

John Fisher Garrett, his wife and their baby daughter Susan Elizabeth Garrett (born 23rd February 1837) moved into the newly-built Parsonage House in 1838. The house was on the site of an old church house, which was deemed to be 'a small house fit for a decent labourer but not fit for a clergyman'. (Burnet, 2010.)

However, tragedy was to strike the following year with the death of their daughter Susan who died of scarlet fever on 16th November 1839 aged just 2 years 9 months. She was buried just inside the entrance to Youlgreave churchyard. (Fig. 3)

Fig. 1

The Old Rectory, formerly Parsonage House.

Rhoda's parents were married on 19th January 1836, at Elton Church, and spent the first couple of years of married life at a house located to the north-east of the village at the bottom of Dudwood Lane. It was during 1836 that John Fisher Garrett was ordained as the perpetual curate of Elton. The previous incumbent was Elizabeth Henzey Garrett's father, Benjamin Pidcock, who had also been the vicar of Youlgreave. Benjamin Pidcock died on 28th August 1835 just a few months prior to the wedding of his daughter.

There is a fascinating and controversial story regarding both Elton and Youlgreave churches that involved Rhoda's grandfather, Benjamin Pidcock, and the medieval font with the stoup. The story goes as follows:

Most of the villagers of Elton were poor miners and farmers living in small cottages but, during the first half of the 18th century, the discovery of rich veins of lead ore brought wealth to the village. Until the early 19th century, the medieval church of St Margaret stood on the site of the present church of All Saints. Over the years, the original structure became unsound and it is said that the mining for lead underneath the foundations contributed to this instability. In 1805, the spire collapsed onto the roof of the nave and it was decided to demolish the church and build a new one.

The Norman font, dating from about AD1150 was removed to the churchyard. However, when the new church was completed in 1816, the font wasn't placed inside the new church but remained in the churchyard until 1833. Benjamin Pidcock was not only the vicar of Youlgreave, but also perpetual curate of Elton from 1811. Therefore, he acquired the font as an ornament to put in his vicarage garden in Youlgreave as, apparently, the residents of Elton didn't realise the font's true value.

The reason for the controversy is that this font is the only medieval one in England with a stoup – see Fig 2. The design of the font is very unusual as it has a stoup (projection) at the side of the font for holding a bowl. There is an upside-down creature, thought to be a salamander, holding the stem of the stoup. The salamander in medieval times was a symbol of purification and enduring faith and believed to be capable of extinguishing fire.

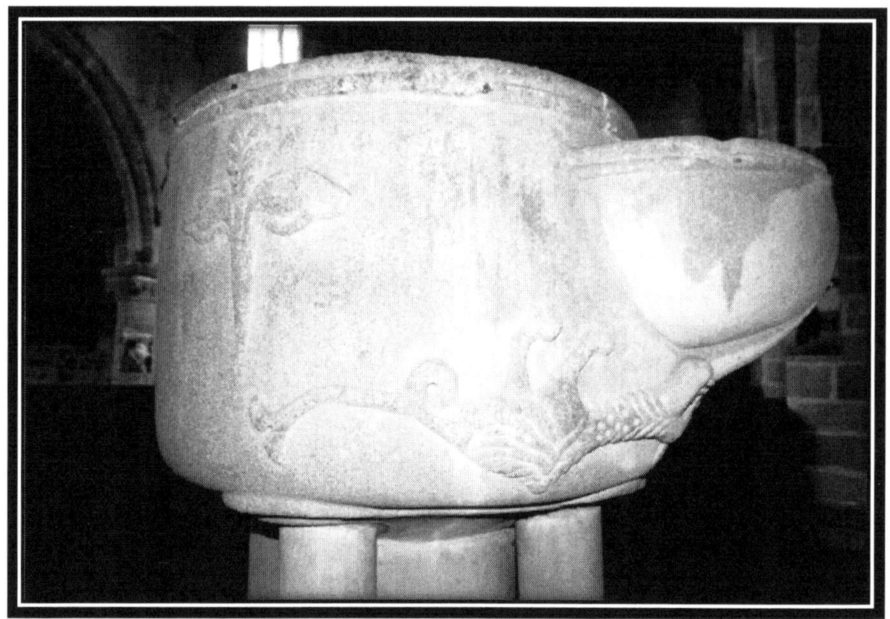

Fig. 2 The Elton Font with stoup, now situated in Youlgreave Church.

There are conflicting accounts of the story of how the font found its way to Youlgreave. It is said in Elton that Benjamin Pidcock's helpers came to Elton in the dead of night to take the font – how could they stoop so low! However, in Youlgreave it is said that the people of Elton had little intelligence and didn't realise the true worth of the font so were only too willing for Benjamin Pidcock to take it to Youlgreave. I will leave it for the reader to decide which version of the incident they believe.

Suffice to say, when the Reverend Wilmot (Benjamin Pidcock's successor) had the font installed in Youlgreave Church in 1838, the people of Elton realised the value of the antiquity taken from them and demanded its return.

It is at this point, remembering that John Fisher Garrett had not that long since married Benjamin Pidcock's daughter, that the situation would have been awkward to say the least for the family. It wasn't until 1870, some seventeen years after the death of his wife, Elizabeth Henzey Garrett, that John Fisher Garrett wrote a letter to the churchwardens of Youlgreave Church, signed by him and 44 Elton residents and freeholders, asking for the return of the font and offering £5 towards a replacement for Youlgreave. This request was denied.

Rhoda Garrett would have been very aware of the controversy when she was growing up.

As a result of this decision, the then lord of the manor, William Pole Thornhill, had an exact replica of the font made for the parishioners of Elton. (Stone, 2016.)

Both fonts can still be seen in their respective churches and, despite the length of time since the incident, the feelings still run high between the two villages.

We now return to Rhoda's family. The next child born to John Fisher Garrett and Elizabeth Henzey Garrett was a son called Samuel Roland Garrett in October 1838, followed by Rhoda in 1841 and finally Frank Burton Garrett in January 1844. The name Burton came from Rhoda's maternal grandmother, Anne Burton, who married Benjamin Pidcock in Kirk Ireton on 4th May 1795.

The census returns of 1851 record that Parsonage House had been enlarged by this time and the occupants of the house included Anne Shackleton, from Hull, the family governess; Elizabeth Stone, the cook; and a housemaid called Ann Smith, both from the village. Also staying were a cousin of the curate, Charles Garrett Shorten, aged six, and his friend, William Samuel Robert Catt, aged eight, both from Suffolk. Charles was the son of Charles Thomas Shorten (1822-1883) who married Elizabeth Susannah Garrett (born in 1819) at Elton Church on 27th July 1843. William Samuel Robert Catt was the son of William Catt (1818-1871) and Henrietta Hephzibah Shorten (b 1820). Henrietta was Charles Thomas Shorten's sister. (1851 England Census, Elton, Derbyshire. HO107: Piece2150: Folio38: Page1, 2005.)

The relationship between John Fisher Garrett and Elizabeth Susannah Garrett was as follows:

Elizabeth was the granddaughter of Richard Garrett of Leiston (1755-1839) who was a brother of John Fisher Garrett's father, Harmon Garrett.

In 1853, tragedy was again to hit the Garrett household. The Garrett children, Samuel Roland, aged 14; Rhoda, aged 12; and Frank Burton, aged nine, were left motherless when Elizabeth died on 18th October 1853. She is buried next to her first daughter Susan in Youlgreave graveyard. (Fig. 4)

Fig. 3 (left) The gravestone of the infant Susan Elizabeth Garrett (Rhoda's older sister).

Fig. 4 (right) Elizabeth Henzey Garrett's gravestone, situated next to her daughter's in Youlgreave Churchyard.

(Note – on Rhoda's birth certificate, her mother's middle name was spelled "Henzy".)

Chapter 2
Rhoda Garrett's Ancestry

I will commence with the maternal side of Rhoda's family. Rhoda's mother Elizabeth's unusual middle name Henzey was given to her by her father Benjamin Pidcock to keep a family name going. Rhoda's 3rd great-grandfather on the Pidcock side was William Pidcock (1667-1724) who married Elizabeth Henzey (1675-1744), heiress to the Henzey family of glassmakers of Huguenot descent (de Hennezel) from Hennezel, a commune in the Vosges department in Lorraine in north-eastern France.

The Henzey family were glassmakers who had migrated to England in the sixteenth century. Ananias Henzey, brother of Staffordshire glassworkers Joshua and Paul Henzey, owned the land around the Shinrone glasshouse in Co. Offaly. Ananias was born in Lorraine about 1569 and was living in Kirdford, Sussex in 1590 (he was Rhoda's 7th great-grandfather). More information regarding the Henzey family can be seen in a book by H Sydney Grazebook, Esq., FRHS, called *Collections for a Genealogy of the Noble Families of Henzey, Tyttery and Tyzack*. (As seen below.)

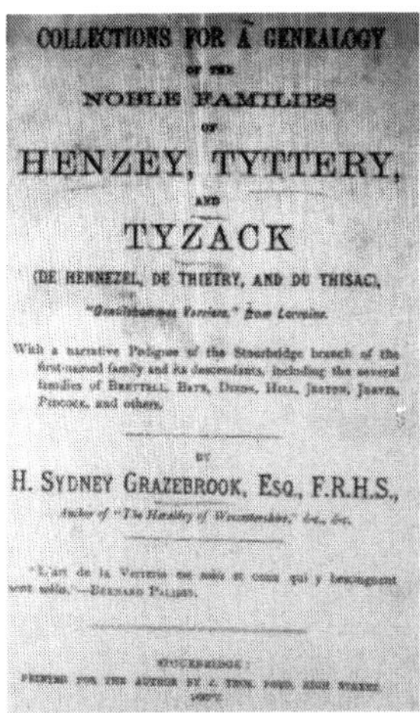

COLLECTIONS FOR A GENEALOGY

OF THE

NOBLE FAMILIES

OF

HENZEY, TYTTERY,

AND

TYZACK

(DE HENNEZEL, DE THIETRY, AND DU THISAC),

"Gentilshommes Verriers," from Lorraine.

BY

H. SYDNEY GRAZEBROOK, ESQ., F.R.H.S.,

Fig. 5 Insert page for Grazebrook's book.

Fig. 6 The de Hennezel coat of arms.

Fig. 7

The Pidcock coat of arms featuring the acorns as per the Henzey coat of arms.

Rhoda's maternal grandmother was Anne Burton who was descended from a line of Derbyshire gentlemen. Her surname was again used by the family for Rhoda's younger brother.

Rhoda's father John Fisher Garrett's family are much better known. John Fisher Garrett was born in Bramfield, Suffolk in 1803, the son of Harmon Garrett (1770-1845) and Sarah Fisher (1775-1851).

John Fisher Garrett studied at Queen's College, Cambridge, where he was given a sizar to assist with his expenses. Unlike a scholarship, the sizarship was not awarded competitively for academic attainment, but rather on the grounds of pecuniary need. He graduated in 1833 with a BA from Queen's.

To qualify for a living, John Fisher Garrett had to be ordained. A living meant a guaranteed income and home for the lifetime of the clergyman. In order to do this following his degree, he needed a testimonial from Queen's College, Cambridge, vouching for his fitness for ordination. He duly received the testimonial from the college and presented the testimonial to the Bishop of Lichfield. In addition, he was required to make arrangements for an examination to prove his competency in Latin, knowledge of the Scripture and with the Liturgy and church doctrine as written in the 39 articles. John Fisher Garrett was duly ordained in 1836 as deacon and priest in the diocese of Lichfield. He was elected by way of a popular vote as perpetual curate of Elton the same year and minister of nearby Stanton and Rowter Chapels (Birchover). He would have had to discharge his ministerial duties to those villages when travelling between them was proportionately more difficult and dangerous as the state of the roads was much worse. However, the additional ministry would have added to his overall income. He was made the rector of the parish of Elton in 1867.

John Fisher Garrett's yearly income at the time of the 1851 Census was about £72 – in today's terms this would represent the minimum wage! As a comparison, in the early 1800s the lesser gentry had income of approximately £300-£400 per annum and yet he was able to employ a governess, cook and housemaid. (Burnet, 2016.)

John Fisher Garrett was of a genial disposition to those people he knew intimately and when he died he would have been much missed by all his parishioners after his 42 years as the rector/curate. In an obituary, they added, referring to Rhoda, that 'he was father of Miss Garrett, of lecturing celebrity'. (*The Derbyshire Times*, 1878.)

Rhoda's grandfather Harmon's older brother was Richard Garrett (1755-1839) who married Elizabeth Newson (1756-1794), the daughter of a prosperous businessman from Leiston, in October 1778. The Garrett family by this time were well-established in Suffolk as tool and machine makers. In the same year as he was married he joined William Cracey at his forge in the High Street in Leiston. He acquired the business in 1782 on the death of William Cracey. They had a son, also called Richard Garrett (1779-1858), who married Sarah Balls (1775-1858), who was daughter of the designer of the first effective threshing machine. Richard and Sarah had three sons and a daughter. Their first child, Richard Garrett (1807-1866), took over the family business in Leiston, developing and making steam engines, steam rollers, threshing machines and seed drills. Richard was to have a stand at the Great Exhibition; the incredible number of orders he received because of the Exhibition enabled him to build the Long Shop, which was used for his portable steam engine assembly.

The other children were Sarah Newson Garrett (1808-1872), Balls Garrett (1810-1880) and Newson Garrett (1812-1893).

For the Great Exhibition in 1851, Messrs Garrett 'gave to the persons in their employment – nearly 300 in number – a treat they will not easily forget, in an opportunity of seeing the wonders of the Crystal Palace. Messrs Garrett fitted up and victualled, entirely at their own cost, two schooners, the *Margaret* and the *Jane* of Aldeburgh, and had them towed by the steam-tug *Joseph Soames* to London, where they remained a week; the workmen living on board during their stay!' (*Illustrated London News*, 1851.)

The Long Shop was the world's first purpose-built workshop used for assembly line production. The machinery they manufactured in Leiston was exported all over the world.

The Long Shop still exists today as a museum.

Although they were not very close relatives, it was Newson Garrett and his wife Louisa Dunnell's family that Rhoda, her parents and siblings were closest to. Much has been written about this family over the years. Newson and Louisa had 11 children in all but one died in infancy.

Newson Garrett's income was derived from his trade as a wharfinger, maltster and brewer. He had gone into partnership with Thomas Valentine Smith of Thames Bank Distillery, who bought the Bow Brewery and the firm owned 15 public houses, mostly in the East End of London. (Crawford, 2002.)

Newson was well known for developing a malting industry in Snape, near Aldeburgh; he was to become Aldeburgh's first mayor in 1885. (Elizabeth, his daughter was to follow in his footsteps by becoming Mayor of Aldeburgh, in 1908, the first female mayor in England.) However, it was Newson and Louisa's children and grandchildren who were to come into the limelight, especially the female line. This incredible family were to include the sisters, Agnes Garrett, Elizabeth Garrett Anderson and Millicent Fawcett.

Of the four surviving sons, Newson Dunnell Garrett joined the Royal Artillery as an officer; Edmund was appointed manager of the family brewery; Samuel, who was Cambridge educated, became a partner in a firm of City solicitors and also went on to become President of the Law Society. His was the first practice to admit women pupils and, unlike his elder brothers, was very supportive of the woman's cause. The youngest son George went into partnership with his father at Snape Maltings.

Rhoda and her siblings in Derbyshire would have been significantly poorer than her Garrett cousins from Suffolk.

Fig. 8 The Long Shop Museum in Leiston.

Fig. 9 Snape Maltings. The site was developed over a period from 1846 by Newson Garrett.

Chapter 3

Growing up in Elton

The 1851 Census shows that Rhoda was being home schooled by Anne Shackleton, the family governess, along with her younger brother Frank Burton Garrett. However, her elder brother, Samuel Roland Garrett, aged 12 at that time, was a scholar living with a relative, George Pidcock (curate of Stonesby Church, Leicestershire), in Chadwell, a few miles north-east of Melton Mowbray.

Rhoda most probably received a fairly limited education as this would have been dependent on how knowledgeable her governess Anne Shackleton was. At the time, one of the only occupations open to women was that of a governess. We know from books written by Millicent Fawcett and letters from Elizabeth Garrett Anderson that Rhoda had been taught to be of a very evangelical creed. She, as the curate's daughter, would have also known most, if not all, the other parishioners of the village. The village was busier than it is now, with lead mining still in operation, having three pubs and a grocer's shop. Now there is no shop and just the one pub. The nearest shop is in nearby Winster.

Rhoda would have also spent some time in the company of both her Garrett and Pidcock relations but most of her childhood would have been spent in Elton and the surrounding area. Elton is the highest village in the neighbourhood and is located high in the hills of the Derbyshire Peak District, within walking distance of Haddon Hall and near the towns of Matlock to the east and Bakewell to the north.

About eight miles south-east of Elton is the village of Cromford, where just 70 years before her birth Sir Richard Arkwright built the world's first successful water-powered cotton spinning mill. This was to change working practices from that time on.

The village of Elton is often quite bleak as it isn't sheltered from the wind and weather. So it is no wonder that the village has a reputation of being cold. Rhoda's father wrote the following in the Elton Parish Register: 'On 9th May 1853 – a very cold & backward season – there was a heavy fall of snow from the N.E. commencing at 5 on the morning & continuing almost without intermission until 7 in the evening. On some of the higher elevations it was upwards of 3ft deep on the level and the roads rendered impassable. Signed JF Garrett, Perpetual Curate.' (Burnet, 2016.)

Fig. 10

Robin Hood's Stride.

Mains water only reached the village in the 1940s, so Rhoda, like other children would have had to take buckets to and from the village to obtain their drinking water from Bury Hill troughs about half to three-quarters of a mile each way from Parsonage House. There was an old well in Well Street, just a few yards from Parsonage House, located outside the churchyard, but this appears to have been contaminated in the 17th –18th centuries. The water from this well could still be used for washing or animals. Rhoda struggled with her health in childhood, a struggle that continued throughout her life. The cold weather and the poor levels of sanitation in the 19th century certainly wouldn't have helped.

Again, from information from her Suffolk cousins, Rhoda loved walking, had a great eye for architecture and form and a love of art. So, with the variety and stunning scenery around the Elton area, she no doubt did a lot of walking, including visiting and clambering over the nearby rocks at Robin Hood's Stride, often referred to locally as 'Mock Beggars Hall' as, like other villagers, Rhoda would have noticed at twilight that the gritstone crags looked like a large house. Just a short distance north of Robin Hood's Stride is Nine Stone Close, a circle of tall stones dating from around 2000BC, although only four are still standing. Just to the east of Robin's Hood Stride, crossing the ancient Portway, which has been in use for over 2,000 years forming part of the long-distance path called the Limestone Way, Rhoda, as countless people both before and after her, would have visited Cratcliff, where a hermit lived in the 14th century, and seen the crucifix carved in the wall of the cave. Travellers along the Portway would have asked the hermit in his cave to say a prayer for their safe journey. (Bates, 2017.)

Fig. 11 View from Dudwood Lane to Robin Hood's Stride (far left), Cratcliff (far right) and below Cratcliff the old Portway path can be seen.

Fig. 12 Crucifix in the cave at Cratcliff.

Nearby Chatsworth House was open to the public during Rhoda's time in Elton and she would have been particularly interested in its architecture and the various internal decorations, including furniture, sculptures and ceilings and the great variety of textiles used throughout the house. Outside in the "Pleasure Grounds", as the gardens were known in the 19th century, she would have seen the gardens at their best, as Joseph Paxton, the 6th Duke of Devonshire's head gardener, created a new record-breaking gravity-fed fountain (The Emperor Fountain), which reached the height of 295 feet (90 metres) and had just completed the Great Conservatory (known as "The Great Stove"), the largest glass building in England at that time; this was the forerunner of Paxton's subsequent masterpiece, the Crystal Palace, erected for the Great Exhibition in London, 1851.

Fig. 13 The Great Chatsworth Conservatory from the Italian Terrace.

As I said in the previous chapter, Rhoda's cousins from Suffolk had a stand at the exhibition but it is not known if Rhoda visited the great spectacle or not. However, we do know that her distant cousins Elizabeth Garrett Anderson and her elder sister Louisa (known as Louie) did.

The village of Winster lies about a mile due east of Elton, and in order to get there you must cross the ancient Portway. Winster is famous for its Winster Wakes. The festivities in Winster have been held for centuries and still occur annually to this day. Wakes Saturday is usually the first in

July unless, if June 24th, the feast of St John the Baptist, happens to fall on a Sunday, then Wakes Saturday falls on the last day of June. Festivities then, as now, include Morris dancing and there are the traditional Wakes Cakes on offer, which I expect Elizabeth Stone the Garretts' cook would have made for Rhoda and her family. Elton Wakes was held the first week in November.

The original recipe is as follows:

Winster Wakes Cakes

1 ¾ lb flour
¾ lb butter
¾ lb sugar
3 eggs
¼ lb currants
One teaspoonful carbonate soda

Rub the flour and butter together and add the sugar and currants, then mix to a stiff dough with beaten egg. Knead a little, roll out, and then cut into rounds the size of a saucer. Place on a greased tray and bake in a moderate oven until a pale golden brown. (Hughes, 2017.)

There is also a folk/traditional song of unknown origin regarding the Winster Wakes, which is as follows:

Winster Wakes

Winster Wakes there's ale and cakes
Allton Wakes there's trenchers
Birchouer Wakes there's knives and forks
Sheldon Wakes there's wenches

This is it and that is it
And this is a Morris dance, sir
Me father fell and broke his leg
And so I took a chance, sir

I dunna know, you dunna know
What fun we had in Bamton
Piece of beef and an old cow's head
And pudding baked in a lantern

My new shoone they were so good
I could dance the Morris if I would
And if in a hat and coat be dressed
I'll dance the Morris with the best

Morris dance is a pretty tune
Lads and lasses plenty
Every lad shall have his lass
And I'll have four and twenty

A toast let's call to one and all
And new ones we're befriending
There's none so dear as them right here
And a song that's near ending

In line 2 of the song, Allton is the present-day Elton and in line 3, Birchouer is the village of Birchover.

Chapter 4
Rhoda and her two brothers

For the next seven years of her life, between the ages of 12 and 19, Rhoda was now growing up without her mother; very little is known about this time in her life, except her schooling at home, Sunday school and visits to relatives. All this was to change when, in 1860, her widowed father re-married 28-year-old Mary Gray, a governess from Grantham. They were married in Rugby, Warwickshire, on 10th April 1860. Mary Gray was half John Fisher Garrett's age at the time of their marriage and only nine years older than Rhoda. This must have been very difficult for Rhoda and her two brothers. Millicent Fawcett wrote of this chapter in Rhoda's life in her book, *What I Remember*, saying, 'Rhoda was a little older than we were [Agnes and herself], of brilliant capacity and great personal attractiveness, witty and very ready with her wit. Her mother had died in her early childhood, and after several years of widowhood her father had married again, and a fairly rapid succession of babies appeared once more in the Elton Rectory. The three children of the first marriage were almost by force of circumstances pushed out of the parent nest.' (Fawcett, 1924.)

Her two brothers moved out of Parsonage House shortly after the marriage. Rhoda's elder brother Samuel Roland Garrett, aged 22 in 1860, went to New Zealand as a colonist during the 1860s and lived there for the rest of his life. It is unlikely that Rhoda was to ever see him again.

New Zealand history at this time was very turbulent. In the late 1830s, growing numbers of British migrants arrived in New Zealand, planning extensive settlements. Large-scale land transactions with the Māori were taking place and there was unruly behaviour by some settlers. The British Government was initially unwilling to act. However, they eventually realised that annexing the country could protect the Māori, regulate British subjects and secure commercial interests.

Thus, New Zealand's founding document, the Treaty of Waitangi was signed on 6th February 1840. This day is now a public holiday in New Zealand. The treaty is an agreement, in Māori and English, which was made between the British Crown and about 540 Māori chiefs (Rangatira). Forty of those chiefs signed that day and another approximately 500 chiefs had signed by September 1840. Not all Māori chiefs agreed, and in the following years wars took place between British troops and their Māori allies against Māori chiefs' forces who hadn't signed the agreement over disputed land sales.

These conflicts escalated dramatically from 1860 as the government became convinced it was facing a united Māori resistance to further land sales and a refusal to acknowledge Crown sovereignty.

In 1858, the Waikato chief Te Wherowhero became the first Māori King and took the name Põtatau. He was one of the chiefs who hadn't signed the treaty. The government summoned thousands of British troops to mount major campaigns to overpower the King Movement (Kĩngitanga) and also to acquire farming and residential land for British settlers.

Samuel Roland Garrett was one of these European settlers (Pãkehã) who worked as a surveyor and civil engineer in the Wanganui district of North Island. He was to become involved in Titokowaru's war in 1868/9 in this district.

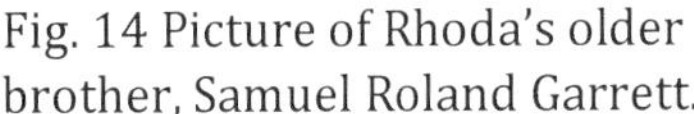

Fig. 14 Picture of Rhoda's older brother, Samuel Roland Garrett.

In February 1916, Samuel Roland Garrett, who called himself Roland, wrote to the *Wanganui Chronicle* regarding the Old Kai Iwi Troop, which had been commanded by Captain John Bryce. He wrote the following about the Kai Iwi Troop that had been composed of frontier settlers:

'Sir, – A short time ago an interesting letter appeared in your columns from an "Old Member of the Wanganui Volunteer Cavalry" of 1868-1869, which brought back to those readers who survive, a recollection of the events of those far-back times. It cannot be expected that the general public of to-day in the face of much more important happenings will be interested in recalling those stirring days, when, as the above writer mentions, the colonists were fighting for their existence, but to surviving members of the Militia and Volunteer Forces of that date it will be of some interest... To account for some of the names also appearing on the Wanganui troop list, I must explain that whilst this corps was intended for the protection of the town and immediate neighbourhood, the Kai Iwi troop was a frontier force, and saw service at various points far up the coast. On one of these occasions members of the Wanganui corps would obtain leave, and join our men temporarily, especially when more or less risk attended these expeditions. These men were therefore members of the Kai Iwi troop for the time being and as such they appear on the roll. Our numbers were made up in a somewhat unusual manner, and though all frontier settlers, we had four Militia officers serving as troopers in our ranks, also our doctor, as we were not entitled to the services of a medical officer as such, so he was exempt from such duties as guards and fatigues, but attended all drills, as an ordinary trooper. We occupied a variety of camps from time to time, some adjacent to the Kai Iwi stream, at all kinds of places up the Coast as far as the old Waihi redoubt in the locality of the present town of Hawera, our duty being to keep open communication between the scattered armed posts and the headquarters at Wanganui. Most frequently when leaving one camp we would not have an idea where we might have to stow ourselves away for the following night, nor where we should procure food for the inner trooper, and as a rule that individual possessed a fair appetite after miles of patrolling on an empty stomach in pursuit of the Queen's enemies of that date, now our trusted comrades. Nor did we confine our attention strictly to the military side of the campaign, as at one period we turned our attention to the naval side and putting our horses in a place of security, did we not take ship, or to be more exact, canoes, captured from the enemy, and force our way some distance up the winding course of the Waitotara river for the purpose of seizing the natives' food supply, and applying the same to our own legitimate uses. In those days our battleships were, I am justified in stating, fully forty feet long, (let the British Navy of this date take note), and were often used as bridges to cross the river, reaching in places from nearly bank to bank. On this particular expedition, however, we encountered no submarines, nor although the navigation was greatly impeded by the Māori eel weirs across the stream, and capsizes were frequent we did not lose one of our men through the action of deadly crocodile. At that time an immensely strong pah existed on the high ground at Nukumaru, overlooking miles of country up and down the Coast. This was, I believe, one of the best fortified strongholds in New Zealand, though the position owing to its being over-topped by still higher ground at the rear was one of the worst. Many efforts were made to capture this pah known as "Taurangaika," and when at length we succeeded, a most wonderful place it proved to be, with its palisades, trenches, and underground passages, and a massive tower of tree trunks fixed upright in the ground, in a double row, filled in with earth between, stood at one corner, called by the pakeha the "watch tower". The site of this tower could still be traced for years after the war was concluded. The list of our old troopers as complete as I am able to make it after so many years is as follows:

Captain John Bryce, dead.	*Lieut. Roland Garrett, Wanganui.*
Cornet James W Baker, Wanganui.	*Sergt.-Major E. James Morgan, dead.*
Sergeant Geo. Maxwell, dead.	*Sergeant A. T. Campbell, dead.*
Sergeant Anthony Rowland, dead.	*Sergeant Ed. Robert Morgan, dead.*
Sergeant John Handley, Wanganui.	*Trooper Philip Mussen (medical attendant), dead.*
Trooper Henry L Peake, dead.	*Trooper G. S. Wright, dead.*
Trooper Joseph Handley, dead.	*Trooper George Peake, dead.*
Trooper G. W. Campbell, Brunswick.	*Trooper John W. Peake, Wanganui.*
Trooper Moore Hunter, dead.	*Trooper W. H. S. Nicholls, Wanganui.*

Trooper Tom Henry Morgan, Hanawera.	*Trooper Alfred Morgan, dead.*
Trooper Anthony Nathan, Taihape.	*Trooper William Lingard, Wellington.*
Trooper L. Wright, Wanganui.	*Trooper George Johnston, Waverley.*
Trooper Robert Kidd, dead.	*Trooper George Mitchell, Westmere.*
Trooper A. D. Cunnabell, Hawera.	*Trooper John N Jones, dead.*
Trooper James Carroll, Kauangaroa.	*Trooper Arthur Wicksteed, dead.*
Trooper John T. Wicksted, dead.	*Trooper Andrew Hunter, Cambridge.*
Trooper A. Wright, Brunswick.	*Trooper Henry G Mussen, dead.*
Trooper Geo. F. Baker, dead.	*Trooper Andrew Watt, Turakina.*
Trooper Robert Evans, dead.	*Trooper Joseph Dyer, not traceable.*
Trooper G. Dyer, not traceable.	*Trooper John Manly, not traceable.*
Trooper Robt. Macally, not traceable.	*Trooper A. E. Capper, Cambridge.*
Trooper William Tomlinson, dead.	*Trooper Joseph C. Nathan, dead.*
Trooper R. W. Littlewood, dead.	
Sam G. Handley, Nukumaru.	*John Wallace, Eketahuna.*

Note. – The two latter were under age and could not be enrolled, but constantly accompanied the troop in the various expeditions, acting as troopers, the latter as trumpeter.

ROLAND GARRETT February, 1916.'

(Garrett, 1916.)

The Kai Iwi Unit was formed in October 1868. The volunteer cavalry elected their own officers; Roland Garrett was originally a cornet, the third and lowest grade of commissioned officer in a British cavalry troop behind the captain and lieutenant. He was later made a lieutenant.

There is one infamous incident, however, that did involve the Kai Iwi cavalry that became notorious, that of Handley's Woolshed in South Taranaki on 27th November 1868. The incident involved a dozen or so Māori children, the eldest aged about ten, the youngest aged between six and eight years, who were attempting to kill a large sow with pocket knives. The noise attracted the attention of the troop who believed it to be Hauhau warriors. The Hauhau warriors were reputed to be the most fanatical, fierce and feared during the New Zealand wars and had revived decapitation and cannibalism during this time.

To the north of Handley's Woolshed stretched well-fenced fields and paddocks, which rose to Titokowaru's new base, Taurangaika. It was on this fateful date that festivities were taking place at the base, with a contingent of Nga Rauru, led by Uru Te Angina, arriving to join Titokowaru's ranks. The men and women were all working together preparing food for a great feast. The only exception was a few scouts keeping an eye out for trouble. Titokowaru had given orders to the elders not to scatter but this did not apply to the children. So the children had ventured out to Handley's Woolshed.

The cavalry arrived at the sand ridge, William Newland (commander of the mounted constabulary) and Captain John Bryce dismounted from their horses and surveyed the scene below them at the woolshed, which was just over half a mile away, they saw some figures in the potato paddock next to the woolshed. They knew they were Māori from Taurangaika. Some of the excitable troopers did not wait for orders and raced for their mounts to charge at the Māori. There were no officers in the leading group. The pursuit was now on, they chased the boys until they got to a big ditch and bank fence, most of the riders were blocked here, but two groups of about five made up of the best jumpers cleared the fence. One group, which included troopers Alex Cunnabel and Tom Morgan crossed the fence to the right but got stuck in a swamp. However, the other group made up of George Maxwell, Arthur Wicksteed, George Peake, Arthur Wright and George Campbell managed to cross to the left, avoiding the swamp and found itself amongst the rearmost children. This group's pursuit was ruthless and at close quarters. It was from this group that the casualties were to arise. Two of the youngsters were killed by bullet and sabre blows and at least five others received sword or gunshot wounds but survived to testify with clarity and consistency at the subsequent investigation. Their translated evidence gave no sign that they held all Pakeha (Europeans) responsible for the actions of a few.

None of the officers was involved. From accounts written, Bryce and Garrett had difficult tasks, Bryce was chasing one trooper's runaway horse, whilst Roland Garrett was furiously trying to get the bogged horses and men out of the swamp before the arrival of the rescuing Māori warriors.

Bryce caught up with Maxwell's group of riders who were in a high state of excitement ready to take on Titokowaru's whole army, who were now almost within gunshot. Bryce ordered them to retire and threatened to cut down the first man to cross him. Maxwell still wanted to go on but was persuaded when he realised some of their own men were stuck in the swamp. It was only then that they went to help Roland Garrett rescue the bogged-in horses and men and retreat to safety. Maxwell was killed not far from the spot where he had killed a month earlier. (Belich, 2010.)

Following the infamous incident, Bryce won a case against GW Rusden, who had claimed in a history of New Zealand that Bryce had 'cut down' women and children 'gleefully and with ease' at the High Court in London. Bryce claimed that he played no part in the incident and the verdict went against Rusden, whose book was subsequently suppressed.

Roland Garrett organised a Public Meeting in 1883 for old members of the late Kai Iwi Troop to attach their names to a letter expressing sympathy for their former captain, John Bryce, whilst suffering under false charges brought against him in Rusden's so-called *History of New Zealand*. (*New Zealand Herald*, 1883.)

Following the end of the New Zealand wars, Roland Garrett, who had been awarded a New Zealand War Medal, was employed as a civil engineer on the Auckland-Waikato railway in 1873. On 30th December 1873, he married Helen Ann Campbell (known as Nellie) of Scottish descent. They had two sons, Roland born in 1876 and Frank William born in 1878. In 1875, he carried out a considerable amount of the original surveying work in the Wanganui district and he was one of the founders of the New Zealand Institute of Surveyors and served on the Wanganui Branch until shortly before his death.

During the late 1880s, Roland Garrett was joined by William Wall and from this partnership today's Payne Sewell Ltd has evolved.

Samuel Roland Garrett died at the age of 82 on 11th July 1919 at his residence, Durie Hill in Wanganui. In the local papers, they'd written, 'Wanganui loses one of its oldest and most respected settlers', adding, 'The deceased gentleman was one of the best known civil engineers in the country, and practised his profession till comparatively recently. He was a man of high principles and was held in the highest esteem by all who knew him.' (*The Taranaki Daily News*, 1919.)

Samuel's eldest son Roland, unlike his father did travel to the Old Country (as they called it in New Zealand) on a mail boat via America in 1906. He followed into his father's profession by becoming a surveyor, but left Wanganui on 20th January 1910, to practise his profession in the Federated Malay States. The *Wanganui Chronicle* described his journey as follows: 'He left Wanganui yesterday for Wellington, whence he sails for Sydney. There he joins the Royal Dutch Packet Company's *Van der Hagen*, which leaves on the 7th inst. for Singapore via Australian, New Guinea and Java ports. At Singapore Mr Garrett will change steamers, going up the coast of the Malay Peninsula to the Perak River, thence going to his headquarters at Ipoh.' (*Wanganui Chronicle*, 1910.)

Roland (junior) was to return to England again in November 1914 and enlisted in the 2nd King Edward's Horse, with which regiment he served for two and a quarter years in France, until it was disbanded. He was then transferred to the Tank Corps and shortly afterwards to the King's Liverpool Regiment. A few months later he obtained another transfer to the Royal Engineers and underwent a course of training at the Ordnance Survey office in Hampshire with a view to a commission in a Field Survey Unit. (*Wanganui Chronicle*, 1919.)

After the Great War, he returned to New Zealand to live. In 1932 he married Myrtle Ruahine Smale when he was 56 years old. He died on 14th October 1954.

Samuel Roland Garrett's younger son stayed in New Zealand and married Sarah Jane Baird in 1902 and they had several children.

Rhoda's younger brother Frank Burton Garrett left the family home in Elton and had lodgings in the High Street, Potters Bar in Middlesex at the age of 17. He started working as a clerk in a bank.

By 1869, Frank had now become a bank manager for The London and County Banking Company at Gravesend and was boarding in the town.

In the *Reading Mercury, Oxford Gazette, Newbury Herald, and Berks*

County Paper, on Saturday, February 12th 1870, they give a list of Persons of whom the Company or Partnership consists for "The London and County Banking Company".

Both Frank B Garrett and Rhoda are named as follows:

Garrett, Frank B., Gravesend, gentleman.

Garrett, Miss Rhoda, care of FB Garrett, Gravesend, spinster.

By the time Frank had become bank manager, the Gravesend Branch was located at a newly-built, more spacious premises, 24 High Street on the site of the old Freemason's Tavern.

Frank's marriage to Adelaide Jane Wasse, the daughter of the late Rev Samuel Wasse BA, vicar of Hayfield, Derbyshire, on 10th November 1875, took place at the Parish Church at St Marylebone, London and was taken by his father, John Fisher Garrett, with Rhoda in attendance. Unlike her older brother, Rhoda and Frank visited each other regularly. Frank and Adelaide had three children; the first to be born was Geoffrey Garrett in Windsor, 1878. Their celebrations would have been hit a few months later with the death of Rhoda and Frank's father on 21st November 1878.

In 1881, Frank, Adelaide and Geoffrey moved to Newport on the Isle of Wight where Frank was still a bank manager. A year later a second child was born on 23rd April 1882, this time a daughter. She was christened Frances Hope Garrett on 28th May 1882 at the Parish Church of St Peter and St Paul, Rustington, West Sussex, whilst the family were visiting Rhoda in the village. However, within a year Frank would have been devastated at not only losing his sister Rhoda in November but also his daughter Frances Hope Garrett at the age of one in 1883.

Frank, Adelaide and Geoffrey moved back up to Gravesend and they had another daughter, Phyllis Gervas Garrett in the town in 1884; the middle name Gervas came from her mother's Uncle Thomas Gervas Esq. from Epworth.

Frank remained a bank manager in Gravesend until his retirement in 1904.

Their son Geoffrey, who was one of the first pupils of Bedales School, founded by his step-aunt and uncle, became a locomotive engineer and their daughter Phyllis married a bank clerk called Bentham Gates. Phyllis and Bentham had a daughter called Evelyn Joy, born in 1910; she became a missionary nurse in Peru.

On Frank's retirement, he and Adelaide moved back to Derbyshire to live at Great Oddo House in Winster, just a couple of miles from his birthplace.

Frank Burton Garrett died after suffering from a weak heart at their house in Winster on 3rd July 1924 and was buried at St Helen's Churchyard in Darley Dale, Derbyshire, not far from Winster and Elton. He was to leave £5,601 18s 5d to his wife for life and then to his children. (The equivalent of about £300,000 in today's money.)

Adelaide died on 1st September 1938 in Cranbrook, Kent, where she had been living since 1926.

Chapter 5
The 1860s

During the early 1860s life changed dramatically in Elton for the Garretts when, after several years of widowhood, in April 1860, Rhoda's father was to marry Mary Gray. Their much loved first child, Rhoda's half-brother, John Fergusson Garrett was born and baptised in January 1861 in Grantham, Lincolnshire. Four further children were to be born at Parsonage House and baptised in Elton church. They were: Mary Amy Garrett, who was baptised on 22nd June, 1862; Fydell Edmund Garrett, who was born on 20th July, 1865; and finally, the twins Elsie Garrett and John Herbert Garrett who were born on 25th April, 1869.

John Fergusson Garrett died at the age of six of a weak heart. A memorial window is dedicated to him behind the altar of the parish church in Elton. He is buried alongside both his parents in the churchyard enclosed by iron railings. (Fig. 15)

Fig. 15 Elton Graveyard.

The grave of John Fergusson Garrett is marked by a gritstone cross. His parents are both buried under the coped stone.

Parsonage House (The Old Rectory) can be seen in the background.

By the time the remaining children were born Rhoda would have been in her twenties and would have had little to look forward to except helping to bring up the children from the second marriage.

Rhoda, as we said, was well acquainted and friends with all her cousins in Suffolk and they treated her like another sister. Louisa, known as Louie, was the eldest daughter, born in 1835, of Newson Garrett and Louisa; she was to go on to marry James Smith. The next eldest was Elizabeth Garrett; she was five years older than Rhoda and, like Louie, was becoming very concerned about the welfare and future of Rhoda. The next daughter was Alice, born a year after Rhoda; she was to move out to India with her husband Herbert Cowell between 1863 and 1872. There were eight other brothers and sisters of Louie and Elizabeth, of these Rhoda was especially close to both Agnes and Millicent. Agnes was the fourth daughter, born in 1845; they lived and worked together both at 2 Gower Street in London and at their holiday home for the summer months, "The Firs" in Rustington, West Sussex. Millicent, who was born in 1847, went on to marry the blind postmaster general and MP Henry Fawcett and was to spend a lot of time with Rhoda in the early years of the women's suffrage campaign.

Elizabeth Garrett, like her brothers and sisters, always referred to Rhoda as "Rose". Elizabeth had realised that Rose was facing the classic old problem of being a semi-educated daughter of a poor clergyman with no real prospects of a decent employment. Elizabeth Garrett had a friend that she confided in, her name was Emily Davies, and Emily greatly encouraged Elizabeth in her medical studies. Emily Davies was an early advocate of women's rights and was a founder member of the women's discussion group, "The Kensington Society", along with Barbara Bodichon; her sister-in-law Sylvia Llewellyn Davies; Dorothea Beale; Frances Mary Buss; and Elizabeth Garrett, and was involved in organising John Stuart Mill's 1866 petition to the British Parliament for women's suffrage, which was signed by Elizabeth Garrett. Emily Davies was also associated with Rustington; her brother Arthur Llewellyn Davies married Sylvia du Maurier and their sons all lived in the village and were to become the real "Darling" family, the inspiration of *Peter Pan* by JM Barrie.

Elizabeth wrote to Emily on 30th Nov 1861 from 22 Manchester Square, London, saying:

'...I am so anxious just now to get Rose Garrett away from home. She can do nothing there, & her parents are willing to let her go. She is fit for very little now, & will have to support herself sooner or later; as they would not permit anything like a manual employment or a situation in an office or a shop. Even if she were fit to take one, wh[ich] she is not, there seems to be nothing but teaching to go to. She therefore wants to get a situation as junior teacher in a school, where she would have some advantages in return for what she has to give – or failing this, she would accept a nursery governess' situation for the sake of making a start. I suppose you don't know any one who would be glad to have her in either of these capacities? She is fond of children & has a good deal of general brightness & general ideas, as Miss Snowdon says, and a freshness of character which makes one hope that she will develop into something more some day. She is very Evangelical in creed, but this is the result of education, & has not done any serious harm. She is very truthful…' (Garrett, 1861.)

The following week Elizabeth wrote to her mother Louisa about a forthcoming visit to Blackheath School to see Agnes and Millicent in which she said she meant 'to take the opportunity of talking about Rose, in case any arrangement could be made for Mrs Hobbs to receive her & give her some instruction in return for services. I am going pretty often to Harley St to inspect the books there for her, but at present nothing has come of it. We have written (or rather she has written & I have sent) several letters, in answer to advertisements but where there are so many well-educated women wanting the situations, poor Rose with her modest "English & rudiments of French & music" has no very great chance.' (Crawford, 2002.)

Rhoda did spend time at the Blackheath School whilst her cousins Millicent and Agnes were there. However, Elizabeth Garrett had her doubts about Rhoda being a successful governess; this she stated to her sister Alice saying, 'She seems to be getting on very well with Mrs Hobbs, and to be liked by the others... Miss Thomas said to Agnes that if she [Rhoda] intended to be a governess "she ought to be a scholar at a good school for at least 2 years, as she could not teach what she did not know".'

A few months later, on the 1st February 1862, Elizabeth said as much in a letter to her mother stating, 'I am sure I don't know about Rose. I have not much hope of her ever being a first or even second class governess but there are many things to make the photography not quite the thing for her. It would be so different if her parents were living in Town but there would not be much saved out of 16/- [shillings] a week when she has to be boarded... I don't wish to suggest it at present but to wait & watch Rose in her present work. I am daily more convinced that trustworthy & trained women can always get work.' The mention of photography in the letter is because at the time there were plans to start a class in photography for women.

It is not clear if Rhoda's poorly paid father could fund her stay at the Blackheath School, but it appears that Elizabeth's elder sister Louie came to the rescue of Rhoda by arranging and financing a stay to Gebweiler in Alsace (The Germanic region of France) for a short time to learn both French and German in an attempt to make her more employable. This region lies on the west bank of the Rhine and has passed between both France and Germany in the past couple of centuries.

Rhoda visited Louie on her way to Germany; Louie mentioned the following in a letter to her mother: '... did I tell you that Rose is coming here on Monday on her way to Germany. She is going by Hamburgh and I believe is to do the greater part of her journey up the Rhine afterwards.' (Crawford, 2002.)

On Rhoda's return from the Alsace, Millicent wrote in her book, *What I Remember*: '...that she came for further tuition in English subjects to Miss Browning's school at Blackheath,' and added, 'She immediately became my guide, philosopher and friend, and more particularly my protector, if she thought there was anything in the school management that was not satisfactory so far as I was concerned. She was far more ready than I was to perceive occasions for her active intervention. I might even have resented her aid if it had not been that she had such a pleasant way with her that it was impossible to take offence or to withstand her.

Our school friendship, and especially that which Rhoda formed with Agnes, almost at the same time had important consequences.' (Fawcett, 1924.)

So, with the help of both Elizabeth and Louie, Rhoda succeeded in acquiring the additional knowledge needed to find employment. It is known that Rhoda was working in Lichfield as a governess in 1864 but it is not known for how long she remained as such. Her powerful personality and her quest for knowledge and training that her family and friends have remarked on would have certainly been an asset so it is not surprising that Rhoda was not content with a career as a governess.

In 1865, Louie and her husband James Smith took Millicent to hear an election speech by John Stuart Mill about trying to extend the franchise to working men and also to women; he was duly elected as the Liberal MP for the City of Westminster. For the Garrett sisters and Rhoda this speech on women's suffrage would have a significant effect. How this would have resonated with Elizabeth who, at the time, was being frustrated at every turn trying to get into the medical profession. She had found a loophole in the Society of Apothecaries that didn't specifically forbid women from taking their examinations; these exams she duly passed and gained a diploma which enabled her to become a medical practitioner. The society consequently changed its rules, stopping other women from entering the profession this way.

The following year John Stuart Mill, now an MP, presented the first mass women's suffrage petition to the House of Commons on 7th June 1866. The petition had been organised by what became known as the "Kensington Committee" who met at the house of Elizabeth Garrett. The petition had been brought to Westminster Hall by Elizabeth Garrett LSA (who had now with her father's backing opened and was attendant of the St Mary's Dispensary for Women and Children in London) and her friend Emily Davies; however, to avoid attention they had concealed the petition under a stall of a nearby apple seller, which is where John Stuart Mill found it.

The wording of the petition, which had 1521 signatories went as follows:

The humble petition of the undersigned,

Sheweth,

That it having been expressly laid down by high authorities that the possession of property in this country carries with it the right to vote in the election of representatives in Parliament, it is an evident anomaly that some holders of property are allowed to use this right, while others, forming no less a constituent part of the nation, and equally qualified by law to hold property, are not equally able to exercise this privilege.

That the participation of women in the Government is consistent with the principles of British Constitution, inasmuch that women in these islands have always been held capable of sovereignty and women are eligible for various public offices.

Your petitioners therefore humbly pray your honourable House to consider the expediency of providing for the representation of all householders, without distinction of sex, who possess such property or rental qualification as your honourable House may determine.

And your Petitioners will ever pray.

Barbara Bodichon; Mentia Taylor; Emily Davies; ... &c ... &c ... (UK Parliament, 1866.)

John Stuart Mill spoke on the petition on 17th July 1866 and a year later the first debate took place in Parliament on votes for women. However, the vote was lost 73 votes to 196 when he proposed changing the word 'man' to 'person' in the 1867 Reform Bill.

The year 1867 was to be a pivotal year for Rhoda. The year started horribly. On 20th February 1867, her eldest cousin Louie, who had been so helpful to her, was to tragically die from appendicitis aged just 31. She had been the Honorary Secretary of the London [National] Society for Women's Suffrage, which had been formed early in 1867. Louie's death was to cause endless stress in the Garrett family. Louie was one of the few people who Elizabeth turned to for advice. Rhoda was to suffer further distress the following month with the death of her 6-year-old half-brother John Fergusson Garrett on March 27th. (See earlier in the chapter).

Yet there was to be happier news in the Garrett family with the marriage of nineteen-year-old Millicent Garrett to the tall imposing figure of Henry Fawcett. Henry Fawcett had previously been blinded, in 1858, accidentally by a shot from his father's gun while they were out hunting. He was the Liberal MP for Brighton and was amongst the small group of MPs led by John Stuart Mill to campaign for votes for women; he was also Professor of Political Economy at Cambridge. The couple were married on Tuesday 23rd April 1867 at 10.30am in the parish church at Aldeburgh. In consequence of the recent bereavement in the family of the bride, the wedding was not marked either by the family or by the townspeople of Aldeburgh with so much rejoicing as would otherwise have been exhibited. Despite this, many flags were hoisted in houses around Aldeburgh in honour of the event and the church was densely crowded with many spectators assembled outside. Rhoda had the honour of being one of the bridesmaids along with Millicent's sisters Agnes and Josephine and Miss Fawcett the sister to the professor. Millicent was attired in white satin, a wreath of orange blossoms and tulle veil, whereas Rhoda and the other bridesmaids wore white embroidered grenadine, trimmed with white satin veils, their wreaths being of white and green flowers. Once the service had concluded, the newly married couple and the family (totalling twenty-two people) went back to Alde House to partake of a very choice dejeuner (as they used to call it). (*Chichester Express and West Sussex Journal*, 1867.)

Fig. 16

Millicent and her husband Henry Fawcett MP on their wedding day.

As described in *The Cambridge Independent Press* on 27th April 1867, 'During the morning the whole of the family sat as a group, which was photographed by Mr JC Clarke in a most effective manner, the posing and general composition of the picture being unusually good and the portraits thoroughly life-like.' Unfortunately, I have not been able to trace a copy of this picture. However, there is a photograph by the same photographer showing the bride and groom on their wedding day. (See Fig. 16.)

There were a very large number of wedding presents from friends and family of the bride and bridegroom including a beautifully carved oak reading desk, surrounded by an illuminated inscription from Rhoda.

Not long after the wedding, Rhoda, who was now 26 years old, went to London intending to train as an architect but was unable to find a practice willing to take her on, as this was a profession that was deemed unsuitable for women. However, Rhoda had kept in contact with her younger brother Frank and was working with him at Gravesend in 1870 for The London and County Banking Company. So at least she was in employment.

Elizabeth at the time was also determined to find a situation for Agnes, now aged 22, as she would now have been the eldest of the unmarried sisters in the Garrett household in Aldeburgh. I will not dwell at length on Agnes's situation during this period as this has been superbly described in Elizabeth Crawford's book, *Enterprising Women – The Garretts and their Circle*. Suffice to say that she was determined to join Rhoda in her quest.

How frustrating it must have been for the two cousins over the next few years.

Millicent Fawcett had written to John Stuart Mill in early 1871 asking if there was a position for Rhoda as a paid secretary for the Land Tenure Reform Association (Mr & Mrs Fawcett were regular dining partners with JS Mill). He replied to her on 26th March 1871, indicating that having a paid secretary would lead to the association becoming bankrupt unless sufficient subscriptions come in. JS Mill also inferred that if Rhoda was to ask say £50 per annum for her services (the late secretary asks £100) then it may be possible if the required subscriptions covered the half.

On 2nd April 1871, when the census was taken, Agnes is shown as still living at home with no employment status. However, Rhoda was lodging at 96 Warwick Street (now Warwick Way), Pimlico, London and working as an editor of newspapers and as a private secretary.

In the late 1860s Rhoda also took an active part in the agitation led by Mrs Josephine Butler along with Elizabeth Wolstenholme against the Contagious Diseases Acts of the 1860s for which she would have been at odds with her cousin Elizabeth who now ran the New Hospital for Women in London. Agnes sided with Rhoda on this matter.

The legislation allowed police officers to arrest prostitutes in ports and army towns and bring them in to have compulsory checks for venereal disease. Many of the women arrested were not prostitutes but they still had to undergo the medical examination. If a woman was declared to be infected, then she would be confined in what was known as a "lock hospital" until she recovered or her sentence finished. It was claimed by medical and military officials that this was the best way to protect men from infected women. Military men were often unmarried and homosexuality was a criminal offence, so that prostitution was deemed to be a necessary evil. The initial Act said that women could be interned up to three months in the "lock hospital" but the later Acts increased this up to one year.

Fig. 17

Photo of Rhoda's lodgings at 96 Warwick Street.

No examinations were carried out on the prostitutes' clientele and this became one of the many bones of contention in the campaign to repeal the Acts, as this law discriminated against women as no similar sanctions were levied against men.

Elizabeth took the view that these Acts provided the only means of protecting innocent women and children from venereal disease.

The Acts were finally repealed in 1886.

Rhoda would always do her bit to raise money for charity; on one such occasion, in September 1869, she was helping to raise money for the parish church at Aldeburgh with her Suffolk cousins. In the *Ipswich Journal* on Saturday 11th 1869, they recorded an extensive report on the bazaar; firstly they describe the village saying: *'Aldeburgh is a very picturesque little town, and it is so pleasantly situated by the seaside as to form a most delightful watering-place. The air is very salubrious, and the shingly beach is an extensive one, being something like two miles in length, and altogether the town possesses many attractions and is a very favourite place of resort during the summer months by large numbers of persons, for whose accommodation many villa residences have been erected from time to time, a large proportion having a beautiful view of the North Sea. As in most other places the sea has encroached considerably, as may be judged from the fact that the parish Church formerly stood ten times the distance further from the sea than at the present time. This Church stands on a high part of the town a good distance from the beach, and it is an ancient and, in many respects, interesting building...'* The paper then goes on to report on the bazaar, referring to Rhoda as Miss Rose Garrett saying, *'The refreshment stall was most abundantly furnished with the good things of this life, and was presided over by Miss Agnes Garrett and Miss Rose Garrett, and these ladies we believe did a good business...'* (*The Ipswich Journal*, 1869.)

Here is an early indication of Rhoda and Agnes working together.

Chapter 6
A New Beginning

Life was about to change for Rhoda in 1871. Back in Elton, Parsonage House had been enlarged to accommodate the larger family and the name had changed to The Rectory.

On February 9th, Rhoda attended the marriage of her cousin Elizabeth Garrett to the Aberdeen-born James George Skelton Anderson (known as Skelton); all the 30 guests were relations except her close friend Emily Davies. One difference between her marriage ceremony and Millicent's was that Elizabeth was not asked to 'promise to obey'.

This alliance turned out to be a useful one for Rhoda and Agnes in their search for training in their chosen trade. The cousins started as apprentices a few months later in the office of Daniel Cottier.

So how were the apprenticeship fees paid for? Agnes would have had a modest income from her family, but Rhoda's circumstances were completely different; she had from necessity been having to earn a living from the age of 20. Perhaps, Rhoda's younger brother Frank, the bank manager, aided her or there was help from her cousin's family.

Daniel Cottier was a Scot who had trained in Glasgow as a glass painter before attending night classes in London under the tutelage of Ford Maddox Brown, where he was particularly interested in William Morris's colour harmonies. When Cottier went back to Scotland he worked in houses and churches around Aberdeen where his reputation for fine work would have no doubt been known by the Anderson family. Whilst he was working in Glasgow he worked with the architect John James Stevenson, a cousin of Skelton Anderson. Prior to Elizabeth's wedding, on 3rd January, she was making plans to alter her house at 20 Upper Berkeley Street, London, so she sent a note to Skelton Anderson saying, 'We ought to go to Cottier soon, he is slow and unpunctual like most artistic people even when Scotch. The furniture might as well be ready to come in the moment the workmen go out... Would it be possible & not very inconvenient for you to meet me at Cottiers at 2 Langham Place at ½ past 1 on Thursday. We could have an hour there before I go to the School Board meeting at 3.' (Crawford, 2002.)

Fig. 18

2 Langham Place, the location of Cottier's office where Rhoda and Agnes started their apprenticeship.

So, it is more than likely, given how Elizabeth had tried to find employment in the past for both Agnes and Rhoda, that it was through this connection the cousins were to finally get their break.

They were to remain with Cottier for about a year and a half but there is a suggestion that they felt they were not being taught enough.

In 1873, the apprenticeship was transferred to John McKean Brydon. Brydon had also worked with JJ Stevenson at his office in Glasgow. When he came down to London he was associated with both the practices of Cottier and of Richard Norman Shaw before setting up his own practice in 1871. Richard Norman Shaw was to design Knightscroft House, Rustington, for Sir Hubert Parry and his wife Lady Maude a few years later and, as we shall see, the Parrys were to become great friends with Rhoda and Agnes.

So, Rhoda and Agnes were now serving the second half of their apprenticeship at Brydon's office, which was located at 39 Great Marlborough Street, London, an office he shared with Basil Champneys. The properties numbered 34-40 consecutively on the south side of Great Marlborough Street were demolished along with other properties in the street; new properties were built on the site and these are now numbered 39 to 45 consecutively. The office was situated a short distance eastwards from the Liberty's store. Liberty's opened a couple of years after Rhoda and Agnes were training here.

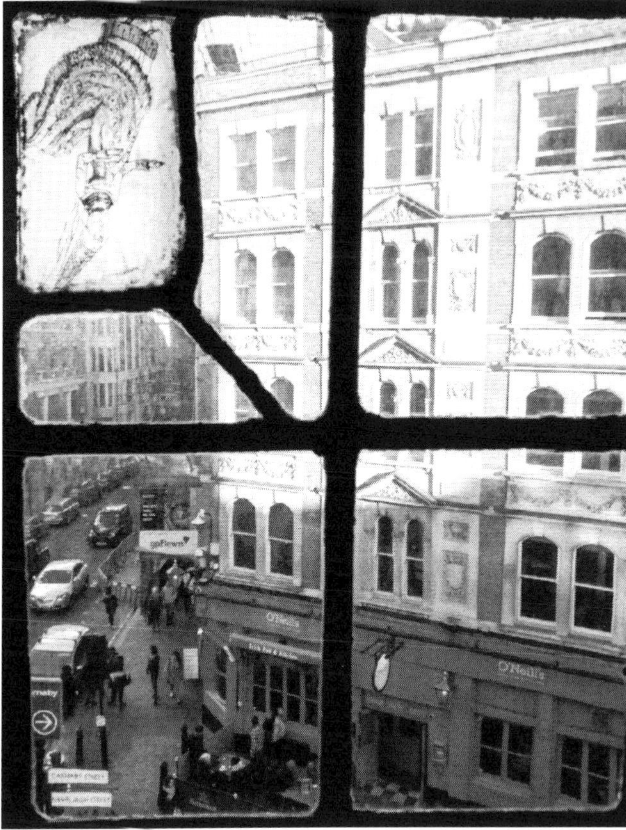

Fig. 19

Looking east from the Liberty's store in Great Marlborough Street to where the Garretts were undergoing their training at number 39. Notice also the lady in the pane of glass top left appears to be upside down.

Whilst the Garrett cousins were working at 39 Great Marlborough Street, in 1873, Basil Champneys was commissioned as the architect for the first building of what was to become Newnham College, to which Millicent Fawcett was a founder. Agnes was staying at the Fawcetts' house in Vauxhall at that time, whilst serving her apprenticeship. So, it would be a surprise if Rhoda and Agnes didn't have some part to play in the interior decoration and design of Newnham Hall. However, there is no documentary evidence to confirm that this was indeed the case. (Conway, 1882.)

What is known though is that both Agnes and Rhoda studied meticulously all aspects of the profession, not just the theoretical but the practical applications. Therefore, the Garrett cousins were later quite adept at not only the design work, scale drawings etc. but also getting their hands dirty, mixing paints, laying gas pipes or even construction of a drain.

Following the conclusion of their apprenticeship during the summer of 1874, Rhoda and Agnes toured England in search of inspiration and ideas. Moncure Conway tells us that when 'their apprenticeship reached its last summer [the Garretts] went on a tour throughout England, sketching the interiors and furniture of the best houses, which were freely thrown open to them', thereby deftly delineating the women as professionals, interested in the antique, and yet of a sufficient social standing that made them welcome in 'the best houses'.

Following this tour, the firm R & A Garrett commenced business!

Not only had Rhoda started her apprenticeship in 1871, but she was also to become a major speaker on behalf of women's suffrage the same year. Her first two speeches were made in Suffolk. Firstly, at the Lecture Hall in Ipswich on Wednesday 12th April and then two days later at Framlingham.

She was to embark on a quest that had first been started in this country by Mary Wollstonecraft in her publication, *Vindication of the Rights of Women*, in 1792.

What these and other campaigners had to endure was not only the ridicule from their opponents but also from the "so-called" unbiased press. I will leave the readers to make up their own minds as to if the latter has changed much to the present day.

Rhoda's first speech was recorded in *The Ipswich Journal* on Saturday 15th April 1871 with a long article under the title "Miss Rhoda Garrett's Lecture on Women's Rights". The meeting was chaired by Mr E Grimwade. The paper started by saying:

'On Wednesday evening Miss Rhoda Garrett lectured at the Lecture Hall, Ipswich, in favour of extending the Suffrage to women. The Hall was crowded, and the audience was remarkably orderly and respectful in its demeanour. We have small sympathy with Miss Garrett and all those with whom she acts, but are ready to acknowledge that the introduction of the feminine element to political life will not be altogether a misfortune if all meetings for political agitation should be similarly quiet and orderly...' They go on to add, 'Mr. Grimwade then introduced Miss Rhoda Garrett, who read her observations in a clear but not strong voice. Indeed we may say that this young lady supplies in herself an illustration of the difficulty – not to say the impossibility of bringing women into public life. We do not argue that Miss Garrett is inferior, far from it, she is a fair average thinker and expresses herself with much more than average precision and elegance of diction, but her physical powers are wholly unequal to the task of addressing a large audience – that is to say if we are to have the audience as well as the speaker satisfied and made comfortable. It is no disparagement to Miss Garrett to say that she has not a strong voice, and we may not perhaps be accused of unduly depreciating the fair sex when we add that were all kinds of professions to be occupied by women we should find a large number of them fail as public teachers for want of the necessary physical powers to make themselves heard by large numbers at a time. We have, however, no desire to depreciate the lady in question. She spoke, or read, which is more trying, for more than an hour, and such the grace and dexterity with which she presented the usual arguments in favour of the extension of the suffrage to women that there were no signs of impatience and the only interruptions were an occasional ironical piece of applause, as some of the bogey arguments were set up ready for demolition...' (*The Ipswich Journal*, 1871)

The *Framlingham Weekly News*, on Saturday 22nd April 1871, reported on the second of the two talks with putting the need to put their own spin on the proceedings and it is from this paper under the title "The Enfranchisement of Women" that I'll quote the speech made by Rhoda on behalf of the suffrage below:

'A public meeting for the advocacy of women's political rights was held in The People's Hall, Framlingham, on Friday evening last. The fact of lady speakers being announced drew a large and respectful audience. Mr Larner, who was suffering from indisposition, took the chair, and he was supported on the platform by Miss Rhoda Garrett (niece of Newson Garrett, Esq.), Mrs. Fawcett, and Miss Agnes Garrett. Mr. Garrett was announced to take part in the meeting, but he was prevented attending through an accident to some member of his family.

The Chairman in opening the proceedings stated that it gave him pleasure to preside over a meeting for the advocacy of women's rights. As matters now are women duly qualified are liable to fill parochial offices – he knew of ladies who were doing so – and he considered it only common justice to enfranchise them when possessed of the same property qualifications as men. He thought the Conservatives would gain the advantage; but justice must be done even though the Radical heavens should fall. He had pleasure in introducing Miss Garrett, who, he doubted not, would ably place the subject before them.

Miss Rhoda Garrett, who seemed perfectly self-possessed, said in opening the subject that she made no doubt the audience was well aware that the women's rights movement was regarded by a large number as a dangerous innovation, by others with scorn, and by many as a subject affording matter for fun and amusement. Of all three classes of objectors to women's suffrage she had, perhaps, the most sympathy with the first, as their opposition was thoughtful and reasoning. There were so many deeply rooted and cherished feelings with which women were hedged round to keep them in their "proper sphere" that he who was bold enough to attempt to make a breach in the entrenchments was likely to meet with formidable obstacles. Those who opposed the possession of the franchise by women urged various objections, with which she would deal seriatim. The first objection, that it is not natural for women to vote, is very difficult to answer, but we must remember that the experiment has never been tried. But as in England it is thought unnatural to vote, so in Asia is it considered unnatural for a woman to go out with her face uncovered; in China cramped feet are essential to female refinement; in Russia women's voices are never heard in church, they not being thought worthy to sing the praises of God in the presence of men. By the old Ecclesiastical law a man was authorised to beat his wife with whips and cudgels, and when it was first proposed to abolish this humane legislation there were doubtless many found to repeat the old Persian proverb that "the stick came from heaven" – in other words – it was natural, and therefore right, for a man to beat his wife. Unnatural generally means only uncustomary, and everything that is usual appears natural. As to the objection that women never had votes, that is tantamount to saying that whatever has been ever shall be, and is an argument applied from time immemorial to all reforms, religious or political. The third objection is that women's sphere was home, and that she would neglect her domestic duties if she gave her attention to public affairs. As Englishmen's home is his castle, but he is allowed to survey the world and mix in its business and pleasures. An Englishwomen's home is also her castle, but in it she must remain, nolens volens, [whether she wants to or not] taking no part in the struggles, excitements, hopes, and ambitions of the world beyond. I know how many will urge against this argument that women like their bondage, that 99 out of a 100 would not change their present happy and comfortable position if they could. That is quite possible, and yet it does not in the least affect the argument. What we demand is that women should be allowed the full possession of their liberty – whether they care to use it or not is always their own option. The liberty to exercise the franchise will not compel women, any more than it now does men, to vote at any election if they do not desire to do so; but the law does not disfranchise a man because he refrains from voting, much less does it disfranchise all men because some will not vote. In this nation there are two-and-a-half millions of British women without husbands, obliged to work for their livelihood. There is an immense excess of women over men in this country, so that unless we import some of the customs of a certain religious sect in America there must always be a large proportion of the female population unmarried, most of whom must gain in some way their own living. But you will ask, "What has this to do with giving women votes!" Much every way, for if a woman has nothing to do with politics, politics have very much to do with her. If women had votes their interests would be better attended to, for no member can overlook with impunity the wants and wishes of a large section of his constituents. Now there are but few employments which a women can follow, and in these it is almost impossible for her to obtain more than the smallest remuneration for her labour. The system of shutting women out from almost all lucrative and honourable employments chiefly arises from men's great respect for social custom and a conviction that the legitimate career before women is marriage. We do not ask for women that special careers should be set apart for them, but that women should have equal educational advantages with men. It would be absurd for women to expect certain concessions on the strength of feminine weakness or incapacity. We say keep them by all means from offices which they should show themselves incompetent to fill. Educate them fairly and train them efficiently, and let them take those positions which require above all things habits of energy, self-control, helpfulness, and industry. You might as well set a man with a wooden leg to run a race with another who has sound limbs as make a woman under her present training a competitor in life's race with men, prepared as he generally is by a training of an opposite character. After contending that intellectual culture was as valuable to the married woman as to the unmarried, in order that she might be a fit companion for her husband, and a fit mother for her children, Miss Garrett considered the next objection on her list, that "women do not want the franchise, for their interests are already sufficiently represented by men". She was aware that a great many women did not desire the franchise, but that went for nothing so long as there were those who did value electoral privileges. No law could be passed obnoxious to the majority provided they had votes, and it was becoming more and more acknowledged that representation and taxation should be co-extensive. At present women were permitted to be taxpayers, but they were forbidden to share in the election of those who imposed taxation. The only other classes from which the privileges were withdrawn were minors, paupers, criminals, idiots, and lunatics. It was side by side with them that men thought fit to range their wives and sisters! They all knew that the majority of women who were happily married neither knew nor cared anything about their legal position, but they also know that not all married women were happily married. Yet by the common law of England everything that a woman had belonged to her husband, and it was only last year that an Act was passed protecting the earnings of a wife deserted by her husband. But there was in the marriage laws a still deeper wrong. Did every mother there know that by the law of the country the custody of her children, after they were seven years old, belonged exclusively to her husband? Even before the 7th year the father had it in his power to prevent the mother seeing them; her only remedy being to obtain an injunction from the Court of Chancery authorising her to see her own children! After seven she could not even demand the interference of the law, and after her husband's death she was not her children's lawful guardian unless by will he made her so. She thought, therefore, she had proved that even married women's interests were not altogether satisfactorily represented by men. Miss Garrett then addressed herself to the next objection, "that women are too delicate and gentle to be brought into contact with the course surroundings of the polling booth". She believed that the presence of women at a polling booth would make it a fit place for them and a fitter place than it is now for men, and that even without the purer and better machinery of the ballot a woman might now go to the polling booth, record her vote, and come away without sustaining any greater injury than a little crushing and perhaps some harmless banter. Women were permitted to vote at municipal elections and school boards – and even to sit up the latter – and also had never heard that the exercise of their powers had in any way unsexed those who used them. It was only in voting for members of Parliament that this mysterious evil influence existed.

They had now come to the much vexed question which had never been satisfactorily or conclusively answered yet, "Whether women are physically and mentally inferior to men, and, therefore, ought to be excluded from political life". Everyone admitted the physical inferiority of women, yet there was no proof of mental inferiority. Analogy pointed the other way. The races of men who had the greatest bodily strength had not usually the greatest intelligence. When woman had enjoyed for as many centuries as men the educational advantages, the discipline of a broader sphere of life, and the stimulus of success for a greater number of years, it would be time enough to enter upon the discussion. At present there were no a priori [in a way based on theoretical deduction rather than empirical observation] grounds for the argument. Whenever funds have been left for education without distinction of sex girls have been excluded by the male trustees, and when public money is voted for education girls are frequently forgotten. Christ's Hospital is a shameful instance of this mis-appropriation of funds.

Miss Garrett went on to remark that notwithstanding all this opposition, the names of many women might be mentioned who had made themselves famous in government, science, literature, and art. Wherever girls had been admitted to examinations in the same schools as boys, as in the Cambridge local examinations, they had proved themselves both able and anxious to avail themselves of the opportunities afforded them. Was not a woman at this moment at the head of affairs in this country?

The seventh argument upon her list was "that if women were to take upon themselves men's work, it would only be fair and natural that men should cease to accord to them those courteous attentions they had hitherto considered themselves entitled to receive". This was indeed a terrible alternative! She did not believe that the cultivation and exercise of a woman's faculties would, in any degree, change a man's feelings towards her, except in increased respect and regard, consequently his manner would denote a truer courtesy, founded upon a more solid and entire basis. It was argued by many that if admitted to electoral representation, women would vote as their favourite clergyman or nearest male relative suggested, but this possibility would disappear as they came to take a more independent and enlightened interest in the affairs of life. Others objected to the dissension which might be caused by the wife having opposite views to her husband, but those whose opinions did not correspond would not be likely, or at least ought not, to marry one another; but even supposing women to be more susceptible to the influence of relations and friends than to their own interests, which she denied, she contended that as the political suffrage was the only means by which rights could be secured, in the name of common justice it ought to be granted to women, no matter what results in the opinion of some might ensue.

To the other objectors, who scorned the subject as a dream of wild enthusiasm, or who looked at it as a good joke, she simply said that the pioneers of all reforms had ever been regarded as wild enthusiasts, and to those who consider woman suffrage a joke she replied that the subject had for ever passed beyond the stage of ridicule. In conclusion Miss Garrett said that the advancement of the question depended upon the energy and steadfast courageous work brought to bear on the agitation. Local Committees should be formed in every town for the collection of signatures to Petitions to Parliament, and for the general diffusion of information. She urged her audience to give to the question the serious thought that Englishmen had never refused to matters affecting the interests of their countryman. All history proved the fallacy of the doctrine that what always had been was always best. Let women themselves prove that the predictions of evil were false, that the more they gained in strength, in thoughtfulness, and wisdom, the less would they lose in gentleness, tenderness, and modesty.

The Chairman said it was intended to submit the following petition to the meeting for its adoption or rejection:

The humble petition of the inhabitants of Framlingham, in public meeting assembled, sheweth –

That the exclusion of women otherwise legally qualified from voting for the election of Members of Parliament, is injurious to those excluded, contrary to the principle of just representation, and to that of the laws in force regulating the election of municipal, parochial, and all other representative government: wherefore your petitioners humbly pray your honourable House to pass the Bill entitled "A Bill to remove the Electoral Disabilities of Women".

Mr Wm. Barley, of Theberton, in a short speech moved a resolution in support of the petition, which was seconded by the Rev T Cooper, and ably supported at some length by Mrs Fawcett.

The Chairman put the resolution to the meeting, when a shower of hands were held up for and only two gentlemen bold enough to oppose. The resolution was duly carried.

Miss Clodd rose to express her great great gratitude to Miss Garrett for her very able lecture; and thought if nothing else had been done than to break down some of the prejudice men entertain towards the subject, much had been accomplished by the meeting. She felt deeply interested in the movement; and it gave her great pleasure to move that a vote of thanks be given to Miss Garrett for her very conclusive lecture. Mr H Goodwyn said, though one of the dissentients to the resolution, he felt pleasure in seconding the motion, which, was put to the meeting and carried enthusiastically.

Miss Agnes Garrett moved that the thanks of the meeting be given to Mr Larner for presiding on the occasion, who she hoped would not suffer from the effort he had made that evening in the proceedings of the meeting. The motion was seconded by Mrs Fawcett, who put it to the meeting, and it was carried unanimously. The meeting then broke up.' (*The Framlingham Weekly News*, 1871.)

Later that month Rhoda was to give a talk at the famous Langham Hotel in London. Rhoda was to go on and make further speeches in the next few of months, including ones at Greenwich, Woolwich, Newark and Leeds.

Rhoda made friends with many of the other leading speakers of the time, one of which was Lydia Becker. She was to go on to share a platform on several occasions with her on their tours of the country.

Lydia Becker, in the autumn of 1866, had attended the Annual Meeting of the National Association for the Promotion of Social Science, where she was excited by a paper from the Garrett's friend, Barbara Bodichon, entitled *Reasons for the Enfranchisement of Women*. Following this, in the January of 1867, she convened the first meeting of the Manchester Women's Suffrage Committee, which was the first organisation of its kind in England.

Lydia Becker encouraged Lily Maxwell to vote in a by-election later in 1867; Maxwell's name had appeared on the list of voters for Manchester. Maxwell cast her vote for the Liberal politician Jacob Bright, who supported the suffrage cause. Bright went on to win the by-election.

Lydia Becker's legal advisor was the barrister Richard Pankhurst, who had also taken a strong interest in legal reform, especially in those laws which discriminated against women. Becker encouraged a further 5,346 other female heads of households to apply for their names to appear on the electoral rolls. These claims were presented at the Court of Common

Pleas by the aforementioned Richard Pankhurst and Sir John Coleridge in Chorlton vs Lings on 2nd November 1868. The case ruled that women could not vote in British elections.

Fig. 20 The Langham Hotel pictured just a few years prior to Rhoda's speech.

(From *The Illustrated London News* – 8th July 1865.)

Richard Pankhurst went on to write the Married Women's Property Act of 1870, although it was changed significantly after it went through Parliament.

In November 1871, Jacob Bright MP attended the Annual General Meeting of the Manchester National Society for Women's Suffrage, where he called for the creation of a central committee in London to co-ordinate the suffrage lobbying of MPs.

Both Agnes and Rhoda were elected to the Executive Committee at a General Meeting held at The Langham Hotel for the newly-created central committee in London called the Central Committee of the National Society for Women's Suffrage (CNSWS) the same year.

The Executive Committee in the first half of 1872 pursued an intensive campaign of public meetings and lectures, which included the issuing of several pamphlets. Agnes became an Honorary Secretary of the society for a while.

In fact, it was at a meeting held in February 1874, at the Free Trade Hall, Manchester, where Rhoda had travelled north to be a main speaker, that a certain fifteen-year-old by the name of Emmeline Goulden was to experience her first public gathering in the name of women's suffrage.

The meeting was chaired by Jacob Bright and the other speakers were Eliza Sturge, Lilias Ashworth and Lydia Becker. (Bartley, 2002.)

Emmeline Goulden went on to marry Richard Pankhurst in 1879; they had five children including Christabel, Sylvia and Adela.

Fig. 21

The statue of Emmeline Pankhurst situated outside the Houses of Parliament. Her first introduction to women's suffrage was a speech made by Rhoda Garrett in 1874.

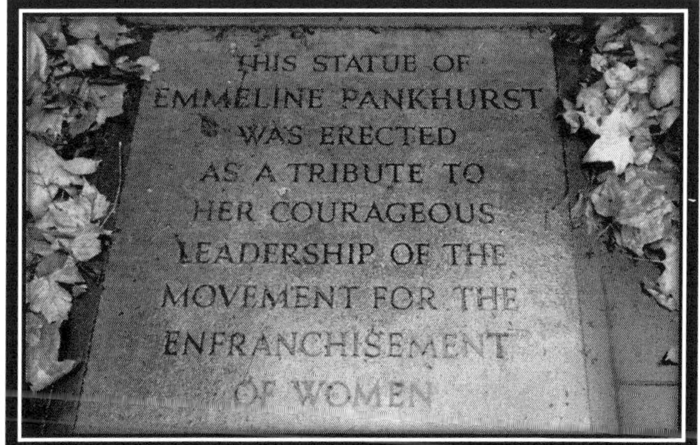

Fig. 22

The tribute to Emmeline Pankhurst below the statue.

Chapter 7

The Royal National Hospital at Ventnor

The beginning of 1872 saw Rhoda continuing her tour of the country giving speeches on the women's suffrage, which included one in Adam Street, London and another in Rochdale.

However, two shocking pieces of news from the village of Elton had reached her in the latter part of 1871. Firstly, there had been a fire at The Old Rectory on 18th December 1871, causing great damage; the property was being enlarged at the time. Fortunately, the family were absent at the time; and secondly, her step-mother Mary Garrett had been taken ill with consumption or as it became better known, tuberculosis (TB).

Mary had been recommended to be admitted to the newly-opened hospital on the Isle of Wight. The Royal National Hospital for Chest Diseases was located at Steephill on the Undercliff, near the town of Ventnor.

The hospital was founded in 1868 by Arthur Hill Hassall and opened in 1869. Arthur Hassall was a British physician, chemist and biologist and was a pioneer of public health regulations and legislation. He chose the site for the quality of the natural environment and he himself put it down as a contributory factor for his own recovery from the disease in 1866. Therefore, he stipulated that the hospital should be in a climate and surrounding that were temperate, with abundant fresh air, sunlight and quiet where persons, especially those in the early stages of the disease could have and experience complete rest to recuperate, receive an adequate nutritious diet to slowly build their weight and with gentle exercise build their strength and stamina – known as the "sanatorium regime".

Mary and other patients attending the Royal National Hospital at Ventnor were also to receive a wide range of medicinal treatments responsive to the symptoms of the disease and these were dispensed by an experienced team of physicians, pharmacists and nurses.

All the patients had their own rooms to avoid cross infection, with individual heated bedrooms and south-facing balcony. This was in complete contrast to the "Nightingale" wards which had been pioneered just a few years earlier. These were named after Florence Nightingale and were to dominate hospitals for the next 150 years.

TB was rife in the 18th and 19th centuries in Britain with approximately one in four deaths in the early 19th century caused by the disease, whilst 50% of those who contracted the disease, if untreated, went on to die of the disease. The disease would normally attack the lungs then spread to other parts of the body. The symptoms being a chronic cough, which could have blood tinged sputum, weight loss, night sweats and fever. It was not until 1946 that the first effective cure and treatment was found for the disease.

The first male patients were admitted in November 1869 and the first female patients in March 1871. Therefore, Mary Garrett was one of the first female patients to be admitted to the hospital. The exact date of her admittance is not known.

So, what did the hospital look like when Mary arrived?

Mary would have been allocated her own bedroom either on the first or second floor in a three-storey cottage along with a basement. There were two cottages side by side in each "block" and these were interconnected by a central east-west corridor. There were eight blocks in 1871-72 (four for men and four for women) when Mary was in residence; these ran from east (female only) to west (male only) and were separated by a building housing a chapel.

The chapel was built and opened the year Mary arrived and there were daily services from a chaplain. Stained glass windows had been commissioned from Sir Edward Burne Jones, Ford Maddox Brown, Sir William Reynolds Stephens and William Morris. Rhoda later would have had direct contact with the renowned William Morris as she sat on the General Committee of the Society of the Protection of Ancient Buildings (SPAB), which William Morris had founded in 1877.

The layout of the cottages in each block was as follows:

The ground floor of each cottage comprised two sitting rooms each for 3-4 persons, separated by a corridor running north-south with the entrance to the block opening onto the north side and Undercliff Drive. All the treatment areas of the blocks were south facing. The sitting rooms with French doors opened onto a veranda, and then directly on into the gardens.

The first and second floors of each cottage comprised three single-person bedrooms – six in total for each cottage, opening onto south-facing balconies. On these floors the corridors again ran east-west with bathrooms, washrooms, kitchens, cupboards and nurses' offices on the north side. All parts of the hospital were strictly marked out as separate to men and women, including the gardens.

In the basement was a subway running east-west connecting all eight blocks with stone staircases to each block and store rooms under the sitting rooms. All the bedrooms were heated with hot water pipes from a central gas and coal fired boiler system. A well was bored and a reservoir made to hold 90,000 gallons. (Eades, 2015.)

Fig. 23

The Royal National Hospital at Ventnor.

Patient notes were kept for all patients at the hospital; they were hand written giving a brief description of the patient's daily condition, the progressive (recovery) of the illness, their weight and temperature, and the prescriptions and medication instructions to the pharmacist and nursing team. These entries were scrupulously maintained throughout the 19th century.

As with Mary, all records commenced with a "Medical Certificate" authorising treatment from the London Piccadilly Office, giving registered personal details of the patient, a short medical history, diagnosis and prognosis, and medical examination report.

Unfortunately, Mary Garrett's patient notes have not survived to this day, although many of her contemporaries have.

The doctors in the 19th century prescribed a series of treatments in the form of:

Tonic – A "lift" of botanical or chemical source dissolved in water.

Tincture – Substances again to "boost" dissolved in alcohol + spirit.

Mixture – Either of the above combined or other additions added to water to produce a "curative" or "alleviate" product, e.g. cough mixture or bottle of medicine apportioned. Syrup usually added for taste.

Liniment – Substances combined and rubbed onto/through the skin. Can be applied as a patch or a "plaster" or "paper".

Lozenge – Substances of bio-chemical source combined with sugar paste.

Pill – Substances of bio-chemical source combined and apportioned.

Drinks – Alcoholic beverages such as "orange wine" or "sherry", cod liver oil, and milk were all flavoured.

There were many medicines used in the treatment of the patients, too numerous to include in full.

These included:

Atropine for night sweats;

Ammonium Chloride used as a cough medicine;

Gold Cyanide – Injections of gold salts for their apparent effectiveness against mycobacterium tuberculosis. This was very toxic in large doses. (Eades, 2015.)

Unfortunately, Mary Garrett lost her battle to TB after an attack of pneumonia on 5th March 1872. The Reverend John Fisher Garrett was so overwhelmed by the tragedy of his wife's death that he was never again able to give much attention to his young family. Rhoda subsequently visited Elton on a regular basis to visit her father and his young family and often had them to stay.

What devastation for the family as Mary Amy Garrett was only ten-years old, Fydell Edmund was seven and the twins Elsie and John Herbert were just three-years old. Rhoda, despite her own delicate health, stepped in to help care for her half-brothers and sisters and she was later helped by Agnes and Millicent.

Mary Garrett was particularly mourned in the village of Elton, the village school having been founded only a couple of years following the marriage of John and Mary, and as the wife of the school's first governor, Mary had taken an interest in the education of the village children, including teaching needlework to the girls.

Fig. 24 The memorial window to Mary Garrett in Elton Parish Church, given by Elton villagers and her private friends.

On the day of Mary's funeral, the village school was closed so that the pupils could follow the procession.

The Royal National Hospital at Ventnor expanded and continued for some 100 years and it was at the forefront of the fight against TB. More than 100,000 patients were treated there, many were cured and others, like Mary, were less fortunate.

The last patient left in 1964 when the hospital closed its doors for the very last time and, in 1969, the blocks were demolished to make way for the Ventnor Botanic Gardens. Virtually the last building to be demolished was the operating theatre.

The area where the hospital once was has now sparked a significant interest from ghost hunters, especially around the site of the former operating theatre, which is approximately where the toilets are in the car park for the Botanic Gardens.

It is believed that the site is haunted; strange things happened when the Gosport demolition contractors, Treloar and Sons, tried to knock down the operating theatre. First, they tried with a crane and a ball but the steel cable snapped. Then they tried a large tracked tractor, three large pieces of masonry fell on it, crushing the cab, smashing the transmission and breaking the steel tracks. In all, four tractors, excavators and a ball were wrecked in the attempt.

Chapter 8
Rhoda Garrett's Lectures

Despite the tragedies happening in her personal life and her own delicate health, Rhoda continued to become increasingly involved in women's suffrage.

Only a couple of weeks after the death of her step-mother Mary Garrett in 1872, Rhoda embarked on a speaking tour of the West Country over the next month or so. These included speeches in Tewkesbury on 19th March, then onto Cheltenham on 3rd April (of which I have attached the full speech below), Worcester 5th, Hereford 8th, Leominster 10th, Market Lavington 12th, Glastonbury 14th and Taunton on the 18th. Rhoda did further lectures in Derby on 22nd April and a famous one at the Hanover Square Rooms in London on 10th May. In late 1872 and early 1873, Rhoda did further speeches including Bolton, Reading, Bath, Bristol and London.

Observing the picture below, Rhoda's appearance is in marked contrast to all the other speakers, showing her strength of mind and individuality. Instead of the shawls and close fitting dresses and corsets worn by all the other women speakers and attendees, Rhoda has her hair loose and over her shoulders, wearing a two-piece, double-breasted jacket with velvet revers worn over a tailored skirt and certainly no corset!

Before giving a full transcript of Rhoda's speech in Cheltenham, I'll just summarise some of the laws that were in place when Rhoda was giving her lectures.

The age of consent was 12 and made carnal knowledge of a girl under ten a felony and of a girl ten to twelve a misdemeanour; also that abortions were a statutory offence. The age of consent was raised to 13 in 1875 and to 16 in 1885 with assaults on girls under 13 deemed a felony and between 13 and 16 as misdemeanours. The age of marriage for a girl was only raised from 12 to 16 in 1929 and for boys at the same time from 14 to 16.

Fig. 25 Shortly after Miss Rhoda Garrett's (standing) lecture in Cheltenham the Women's Disability Bill was thrown out in the House of Commons. Rhoda continued to speak out against these injustices and is pictured here speaking alongside her cousin Millicent Fawcett (seated front left) on 10th May 1872. Agnes is seated on Rhoda's right.

Here is the full transcript of Rhoda's lecture in Cheltenham:

Rhoda Garrett

Electoral disabilities of women

(Rhoda Garrett lecture at the Corn Exchange in Cheltenham on 3rd April 1872)

In speaking on the subject of the Electoral Disabilities of Women, it is no longer necessary to preface one's remarks by an elaborate explanation of what is meant by this demand that we are now making for admission to Electoral Representation. The subject has of late been too widely discussed to allow of any very great ignorance as to the matter to be dealt with in a lecture upon Women's Suffrage; still I do not for a moment venture to hope that this discussion has caused even one-hundredth part of the excitement created by the Tichborne case, for example, though it involves a great political reform affecting not one family alone, but all classes of Her Majesty's subjects. In what manner it thus affects the interests of the entire nation, it will be my endeavour to point out in the course of my lecture to-night.

In order to bring my subject within as narrow a compass as possible, I will divide it into three parts:

1. The education of women;
2. Their economic position;
3. The existing laws especially affecting the interests of women.

I dare say that at first sight you will be unable to see how the possession of the Suffrage by women would improve their position either educationally, economically, or legally; but by the time I have concluded my paper I am bold enough to hope that I may have convinced those who need convincing, that the Suffrage is, as Mr John Stuart Mill says, the turning-point in women's cause, and that with it, they cannot long be denied any just right, or excluded from any fair advantage.

Let us first of all consider the present state of education among women, from the time when they are first capable of receiving any education at all, until they arrive at that happy climax, when they are pronounced by their parents and guardians "finished". In the training of very young children there is, of course, comparatively little difference between the actual teaching to boys and girls, but in their moral and physical training, the difference is even then apparent. Boys are taught from the earliest period of life to be self-dependant and self-reliant; while girls are taught, on the contrary, to be yielding, self-sacrificing, and reliant on anyone rather than upon themselves. A boy is encouraged to develop his physical powers out-door sports of all kinds, and to interest himself in a variety of pursuits, which cultivate habits of observation, and often lay the foundation for a love of natural science which in after life proves most valuable. A girl generally receives training of a very opposite character. If she shows a disposition to join in her brothers' games and amusements she is probably told that such conduct is "unladylike", that little girls should not be "tom-boys", and that, instead of running and jumping and climbing she should get to her sewing and knitting and "keep quiet". I believe it is a generally received axiom that men are more selfish than women, and it is easy to trace the growth of this selfishness in men to that spirit of excessive self-sacrifice in women which, even as boys, they have been taught to look upon as natural, and to regard as a right.

Passing from the home life, let us see how boys and girls are respectively prepared for the work of life by the education given to them at school. Everyone knows how immensely superior the educational advantages open to boys are, to those which are offered to girls. A boy is sent, or at any rate may be sent, to one of the great public schools and afterwards to one of the Universities. In each case his education will be conducted by men of the highest ability and learning. Contrast this with the education his sister is likely to receive at the small private school which is open to her. The teachers here, when they are women, have seldom been trained to teach, and have in nearly every case undertaken the profession from necessity, and not from choice; consequently they are only able to impart to their pupils the smatterings of knowledge that it has been in their own power to acquire. The most important subjects for female education are generally considered to be accomplishments so-called – a little bad French and music, and worse drawing, with a great deal of fancy needlework. If anyone doubts the truth of my statements let him read the School Commissioner's report which lately enquired into the state of education in girls', as well as in boys' schools. Here the evidence is so united and voluminous that my difficulty, in selecting any one part as especially illustrating the poverty and worthlessness of the education now offered to girls, has been to choose, out of so great a choice, not to find suitable matter.

Before I read the quotation I should like to draw attention of those present, who take an interest in the education of girls, to a book which has been compiled by Miss Beale, of Cheltenham, from the reports issued by the Schools' Inquiry Commission; it is most valuable as containing in one small volume all the evidence, and the reports, which were received by the Commission on Girls' Schools. After describing the teaching given in a girls' day school, one of the assistant commissioners says, 'The boarding school, (assuming it, as one may do, to belong to the same class), follows (in all probability), the same vicious system as the day school; and the only difference that it makes to the girl is to take away some of the primitive roughness or simplicity of her manner, and give it an air of affection and restraint. Then at sixteen she goes home "for good". She displays the two or three pieces of ornamental needlework, each of which has occupied her three months, and some drawings, copies from the flat, of figures and landscapes, whose high finish betrays the drawing master's hand. A neighbour drops in, conversation turns upon Jane's return from school, and the mother bids her play one of the pieces she learnt there. For two or three weeks this exhibition of skill is repeated at intervals, and then it ceases, the piano is no more touched, the dates of inventions, the relationship of the heathen gods, the number of houses burnt in the fire of London, and other interesting facts contained in Mangnall are soon forgotten, and the girl is as though she had never been to school at all. There are few books on her father's shelves, perhaps two or three green or yellow novels, some back numbers of the *Family Herald*, Mr Tupper's *Proverbial Philosophy*, Cowper's poems, with gilt edges, more often dusted than opened, *Enquire Within Upon Everything*, and one or two religious biographies. It is not this want of material, however, that quenches her taste for reading, for school gave her no such taste, her life henceforth, till marriage, is listless and purposeless, some of it spent in petty occupation, more of it in pettier gossip; and when at last she is called upon to manage a household she finds that her education has neither taught her anything that can be of practical service, nor made her any fitter than nature made her at first to educate and govern her children. In point of knowledge and refinement, she is just where her mother was, and her sons and daughters suffer for it.'

I must here say a few words on the question of endowments as affecting educational establishments. It is a well-known fact that all the enormous sums set apart for purposes of education are almost entirely devoted to the teaching of boys. The trustees of public educational charities have generally managed to employ the funds exclusively for boys, and Parliament, in voting money for education, has very often forgotten the existence of girls. Where funds have been left for education without distinction of sex, girls have often been unfairly dealt with; as in the case of Christ's Hospital (the Bluecoat School) which was originally established for the purpose of maintaining a certain number of boys and girls. The funds of this school now amount to £42,000 a year; out of these funds one thousand two hundred boys are fed and clothed, and educated in such a manner as to fit them to proceed to the Universities, and nineteen girls are trained as domestic servants.

It must be remembered, moreover, that it is not alone to boys whose parents are rich that all those advantages are open. To every large public school there are attached scholarships open for competition to all the pupils, and therefore any boy of fair ability and perseverance may, by gaining one of them, obtain a sufficient yearly sum to enable him to pay, at any rate, a considerable part of his college expenses, and, when once the doors of the University are open to him, it is surely his own fault if he does not win for himself both honour and emolument.

Where now shall we look for similar advantages for the sisters of these fortunate boys? Referring to the subject, the report of the Schools' Inquiry Commission before mentioned says: 'Examinations and endowments afford, at the present time, the best practical method of improving female education. We can only improve the education of the classes below by beginning at the top and improving the higher education, especially that of the teachers. Here scholarships would be most useful.'

Of course it is impossible to me to point out, in the brief space of time at my disposal, all the evils that must arise from such a one-sided system of education as this – in the one case, we educate entirely for life in the world, in the other, for life at home. We well know that men neither can, nor do, live entirely in, and for the world; nor can women live entirely in, and for, the home. Both are impossible as both are undesirable.

Let us now trace the connection between the education of women and their electoral disabilities. It will be readily admitted that the scope of education is to fit the child for his, or her, future place in the world; and here, as everywhere, as we sow, so also shall we reap. If, therefore, we give to girls such an education as that I have described, is it unlikely that when they grow up they will be both physically and mentally weak, ignorant, dependant and frivolous, unfit, as they are often declared to be, to be entrusted with civil and political rights?

But think you these evils will be best remedied by insisting upon their remaining in this state of dependence, or by admitting them to a broader and a freer life; by giving them responsibility as an educational power? Is it not this what was done for working men in the passing of the last Reform Bill? Was it not argued that none but working men could tell what the needs of their own class were, and that, through their representatives, they had a right to express their opinions in Parliament? Is the same argument less forcible when applied to women?

Would they consent to be excluded from a fair share in educational advantages if they could, in like manner, make their voices heard in the Legislature of the country? Would not their claim to be educated as solidly, and in the same branches of knowledge as men, be argued with a far greater chance of success, if they possessed the power of urging its justice before that tribunal where men are able to lay their grievances, and enforce their redress?

Having now given a brief sketch of the early life and training of a woman, let us see how she is likely to fare when she is ready to take part in the real work of life. In other words, let us examine the economic condition of women. Most people will tell us that a woman has no need to take part at all in the world's work; that if she is all she ought to be, attractive, young, and with an adequate knowledge of cookery and shirt-buttons, some man will certainly wish to marry her, and then she will have no need to trouble her head about politics and the like, with which she has no concern. This is no doubt very plausible, and the majority of women will probably always choose to marry, if a suitable opportunity presents itself; but granting that the greater part of the female population is thus comfortably provided for, there still remains an enormous proportion of unmarried women, most of whom must support themselves by their own earnings. Now custom usually attaches a kind of stigma to what is called an "old-maid", that is to say, a woman who, either from necessity or choice, is still unmarried when she has passed her early youth. But possibly custom might be a little more lenient to her misfortunes, if it were universally known that, in consequence of the great excess of the female over the male population in this country, there are two million and a half of British women without husbands, many of whom are obliged to work for their own subsistence. As, therefore, a great many women are, willing or unwilling, compelled, by the law of this land, that a man shall have only one wife at a time, to remain in single blessedness, it will be for the advantage, both of themselves, and of the community at large, that they should not only be self-supporting, but productive labourers.

I will not here enter particularly into the many difficulties and disadvantages of women of the so-called working classes, simply remarking, as I pass, that the universally low rate of wages amongst them, as compared with those men of their own class, is accounted for principally by the fact that women rarely receive proper training for the work they undertake to perform; consequently, their work is unskilled, and therefore inferior. Even where a woman is able to perform the same work equally well with a man, her labour is not remunerated in the same degree in consequence of the custom I have just alluded to. If a man engages in a trade of a mason or carpenter, or even a tailor or cook, he receives a proper training, and serves a regular apprenticeship; but it is not thought necessary to give these advantages to a woman; at any rate not on the same thorough and distinct understanding. I will give one or two illustrations of what I mean in regard to this subject, and then pass on.

Let us take as one example, out of the many that might be advanced, that of a cook in a wealthy family. If this same cook is a man, he has exactly similar work to perform as a woman would have in the same position – neither more nor less – but he has, in all probability, served a proper and recognised apprenticeship to his trade, and he can, therefore, always command a higher price for his labour. A woman may have exactly the same amount of knowledge; may be quite as competent to prepare those marvels of cookery that aristocratic palates delight in, but she has no credentials from Soyer or Francatelli to assure her employers of her capability; she has, moreover the precedent of custom against her, and therefore, for the same work, performed in an equally satisfactory manner, she is paid half, or at any rate, one third, less than a man would be. Again. A large hairdresser in London has lately (to his credit be it spoken) adopted the sensible custom of employing young women in his establishment to cut and dress the hair of his lady customers. One of the girls employed in this business told me the other day that the women were always paid less than the men. Now this is obviously unfair. The girls do their work most satisfactorily; and their department more difficult and requires more skill than that of the men, for they have not only to cut a lady's hair, but also to construct upon her head one of those marvellous erections with which too many English girls in these days disfigure themselves, and which I am sure it would puzzle their male competitors to fabricate.

These two instances alone will show you how unfairly even the skilled labour of women is remunerated. But I grieve to say there are thousands of women, who through deficient training, have not the same skilled labour to offer, and must suffer accordingly. We do not ask for these that competent, or incompetent, they should receive the same wages as men. What we do ask is that women should no longer be placed at a disadvantage; we ask that they should have as good an education, and as many opportunities as men for fitting themselves for their work; which, with the removal of trade monopolies, will at least give them a fair chance; and then, and only then, can it be justly said that it is their own fault if they do not make their own way in the world as men now have it in their power to do.

But, bad as the economic condition of women of the working classes is, it cannot be regarded as so difficult to improve as that of the more educated middle-class women, who, in addition to a training which tends absolutely to unfit them for work, have to contend with a mass of prejudice against their working at all, which is all the more formidable inasmuch as it is unreasonable, and therefore unconvinceable. The economic condition of such women, their exclusion from nearly all lucrative and honourable employments – their consequent dependence upon men for their support – are evils which increase with the growth of the population, and which the State is no longer justified in ignoring. For an educated woman there is no middle path. Either she must be Queen of England – the head of the State – or she must be shut out from nearly all the advantages of a citizen in a country over which a woman rules. To begin with the offices under Government. The numerous servants employed thereby (some of whom earn, or, to speak more precisely, receive several thousand a-year) are exclusively male subjects of her Majesty; except in the telegraph offices where, through the exertions of Mr Scudamore, women have been admitted. But even here, they are admitted, as Mr Scudamore himself told me, only in the lower grades, where, after years of faithful work, they might eventually earn £200 a-year. The office of superintendent, which women are quite as competent to fill as men, is denied to them, solely because they are women, not because they are in any way incapable of fulfilling its duties. There are many other civil offices quite as suitable to women as telegraphy, though requiring a higher education, for which hundreds of British gentlewomen would gladly fit themselves, the greatest proportion of whom, even the most delicate, would have physical strength enough to read *The Times* daily from ten to four.

The influence thus exercised by the Government in declaring women ineligible to hold office under it permeates through society and countenances their exclusion from the three learned professions – from the Church, where, as teachers of morality their influence and example would be as valuable as that of men; from medicine, though it is often said that it is a woman's special province to minister to the sick; and from the law, where – well, perhaps, some more of that tenderness of conscience, which men tell us is one of the peculiar characteristics of woman, might not be injurious to the higher interests of that learned profession.

Let us now note the difficulties a woman is likely to encounter, if she seeks to enter trade. Here there are no charters, it is true, as in the professions, to prevent her entrance at the very threshold. But there are lions in the way quite as formidable; blind prejudice, on the one hand; and a fear of injuring established interests on the other. You must not think I am drawing a fancy picture – that no woman would wish to engage in trade. I know women who have tried to do so, and whose difficulties lay, not in their want of power to acquire the requisite knowledge, but in the almost overwhelming prejudice of those already in possession of the vantage ground which stops them at every turn. It is often urged against admitting women to a share in the real work of life that they are neither physically nor mentally strong enough to compete with men; but no amount of hard work, with the hope of success at the end, would break down a woman's health in comparison with the struggle with anxiety, disappointment and contempt, which she now has so often to endure, and which truly makes "the whole head sick, the whole heart faint". I do not believe that men mean deliberately to be unjust to women; but they think they are the best judges of what nature intended women to be, and to do, and it must be confessed that, to a certain degree, women have hitherto endorsed this opinion, by accepting with more apparent than real content, the role of dependence and frivolity prescribed for them. The only qualities expected, nay, insisted upon, in women by men, are but too often those declared by Sir Charles Sedley to be the sole characteristics of the female mind:

> All that in woman is adored
>
> In thy fair self I find,
>
> For the whole sex can but afford
>
> The handsome and the kind

But here let me point out that the prejudice middle-class parents, almost without exception, have against their daughters working, possesses a power which in very few other cases prejudice is able to wield. There is no trade which can be entered into without capital, whether a shop of the humblest dimensions be opened, or a brewery established. Years before a boy has left school the prudent father is casting about in his own mind what trade or profession shall be adorned by presence of his cherished young hero. Every taste that he has given the slightest indication of is considered; and even, in some cases, the merits of his personal appearance and manners receive due weight. But the trade fixed upon, the next question which the father propounds to himself is, 'How can I provide the capital, first to article my boy to a respectable firm in the trade he has chosen, and afterwards to establish him in a business of his own?' But though parents thus recognise the necessity of providing for their sons, it never seems to enter their heads that the same thing should be, at any rate, offered to their daughters. Girls never have any capital, they hardly know what it means; yet without it the very first move is impossible; they may enter a shop, but they cannot own one. A boy is considered almost a miracle of goodness if, his premium paid, and his living expenses provided for, he lives morally and respectably, keeps out of debt, and applies himself with a moderate amount of intelligence to learn his business. To a girl, who, without any of these encouragements, plods on her way, eagerly learning the drudgery of some trade in which she can scarcely hope to be a master hand, such a need of praise is rarely offered. The excuse which parents generally give for making such a distinction between their boys and girls is that if the girl married at the end of her apprenticeship, the money paid for her premium would be lost.

In answer to this several counter arguments may be used. In the first place it may be urged, that even if she did marry before she had regained in trade the sum expended upon her training, the business habits acquired during her apprenticeship, and the knowledge of how to expend her money to the best advantage would ensure her becoming the satisfactory steward of her husband's domestic expenditure, instead of (as is now too often the case) the thoughtless and extravagant agent, who is, during the first few months of marriage "chaffed" for her ignorance in money matters; next, angrily expostulated with, and finally deprived of any power over the expenditure whatever. In the next place the advantage may be pointed out, that the girl who has a trade at her fingers' ends, would not be likely to accept the first man who offered himself for her hand, whether she loved him or not. In other words, marriage would not be (as is too often is now) the only profession into which women can enter, and the one position in which society will recognise their right to lead free and individual lives. For, as *The Times* observes, 'At present the language held by society to women is "marry, teach, die, or do worse".' I do not for one moment believe, and, if I did, I should never succeed in persuading you, that boys and girls will leave off falling in love and marrying. I am sure that few men are so modest as to believe that they are likely to find really formidable rivals in dusty ledgers, hard office stools, or even in full cash boxes. So far from this I would contend that the wives they would gain would become wives voluntarily and joyfully, and the more joyfully because voluntarily. Whatever business they were engaged in would either be disposed of, or perhaps carried on for the advantage of the family. Woman now but too often feel that in marrying they are submitting as it were to a fate which they suppose is inevitable; for as Mr Mill says, marriage must be regarded as Hobson's choice – that or none – so long as its only alternative is a dull, lonely life, embittered by the thought of the wasted energies or mis-used talents that, under other circumstances, might have been turned by the despised old-maid, to her own welfare, and to the advantage of the world.

Is there any difficulty now in seeing how the general position of women hinges on their exclusion from the suffrage? Has not representation been the point for which all classes, who have had wrongs real or imaginary, have struggled? Is it necessary to explain what an advantage it would be to many women, now forced to work with competitors, who, at every turn, receive privileges and encouragement which are denied to them, to be placed in this respect, at least, on an equal footing with men? And lastly, is it necessary for me to point out how the responsibility of possessing a share in the government of the country (and a vote does give that share) would awaken from their lethargy those women who are now leading selfish – wickedly selfish – lives of indolence and gaiety; would force them to think out questions to which they now persistently shut their eyes, because they are painful or disagreeable, and would teach them that the souls and lives of their poorer sisters, whom a helping hand might save from despair, or guard from temptation, will be required of them. Thousands of women need only this awakening to be capable of doing noble deeds. 'Women often take meaner things because meaner things only are within their reach.'

Having now considered, as fully as time permits, the position of women educationally and economically, we come to the last point that remains for me to examine. What is the legal position of women in this country? I will speak, in the first place, of the laws relating to married women; and, in exposing their injustice and partiality, I hope all the husbands here present will not think I am having a sly hit at them individually and collectively; at the same time, if, in any case, the cap should fit, they have my free permission to put it on. Of course, we all know that laws are not framed for those who do well; and it is a merciful thing that the majority of husbands have not the disposition to put in force all the power of tyranny and cruelty that our English laws place in their hands. As marriage is the only, or almost the only, career appointed by society for a woman; the one for which she is educated and taught that it is her highest duty to prepare herself; it might naturally be supposed that everything would have been done to make this condition as eligible and attractive as possible, so that she might never be tempted to desire any other. But surely, if women carefully considered what the laws of marriage really are, they would be more likely than when they are absolutely ignorant of these laws, to remain single, and to believe, with St Paul, that "they are happier if they so abide!" Wives in England, are, in all respects, as to property, person, and children, in the legal condition of slaves. When a man takes a wife he swears to endow her with all his worldly goods; then the law steps in and helps him to keep his vow by at once handing over the entire property of the wife to the husband, and declaring her incapable of holding property. Speaking on this point reminds me of the amusing description of the marriage service given by Sir John Bowring. 'Look at the marriage ceremony,' he said, 'it is wicked from beginning to end. "With this ring I thee wed" – that's sorcery; "With my body I thee endow" – that's – that's a lie!' It is true that the richer classes in this country are able, by the costly means of settlements, to set aside the law, and to withdraw the whole, or part of the wife's property from the control of her husband. But even then they are not able to give it into her own keeping – it must be held for her by trustees, and hedged round by numerous perplexing and irritating provisions.

In the Session of 1870 an Act was passed entitled, the Married Women's Property Bill. This Act was supposed to do for poor women what settlements do for rich ones. It was intended to prevent the personal property of a woman, her wages, her savings, and her earnings, being at the absolute mercy of her husband or his creditors. I have not time to enter into all the provisions of the Act, which is certainly a step in the right direction, but unfortunately a very short step; for it does not in any way recognise the only just principle of all legislation, namely, the perfect equality of all before the law. One illustration will be enough to demonstrate to you the kind of justice meted out to women under the new Act, and you shall judge for yourselves whether it is unreasonable for women to ask for something a little better. The case was recently tried in the law courts, and the account of which I am about to read to you was taken from the *Pall Mall Gazette*, a paper which, as a rule, certainly never errs on the side of over-justice to women. 'It is to be hoped,' remarks the *Pall Mall Gazette*, 'that women will not read the case of Shillitoe v Shillitoe, which has just come before Vice-Chancellor Wickens, for it will give them a real grievance with which to make themselves and others uncomfortable, instead of those imaginary grievances that occupy so much of their time and attention. It seems that no settlement was executed on the marriage of Mr and Mrs Shillitoe. At the time of her marriage, Mrs Shillitoe had a sum of £500 at the Selby Bank in her maiden name. Soon after the marriage, at her husband's request, she drew the sum out of the bank on a cheque of her own and brought it home in order to pay rent and other specific sums with it. Two days after Mr Shillitoe died. No rent was paid, and Mrs Shillitoe for the first time ascertained that her husband was indebted to his father and his brother and to other persons, and was so when they were married. The estate was being administered, and she was called upon to account of the £500 as part of her husband's property, without which sum the assets would be insufficient to pay the creditors. She declined to account for, or to pay over the money, and claimed it as her own by right of survivorship. It was insisted, on behalf of the creditors, that there had been a good reduction into possession of the £500 in the lifetime of Mr Shillitoe, and that his widow could not retain it. On the other hand, Mrs Shillitoe's counsel urged that the bank had paid the money to that lady as hers, and would not otherwise have paid the money at all; that it was in equity hers, for if she had known her husband's actual position at the time of the marriage, she would have insisted upon a settlement of the money, and could have done so at any moment if he had refused. If this fund were taken from her she would have only £4 10s, a-year to live upon. The Vice-Chancellor decided that there had been a perfectly good reduction of the money into the possession of Mr Shillitoe, and that the widow must hand it over to the executors. The case was no doubt a hard one for her, but the law – and a most important one it was – was too clear upon the subject.'

Well! This is how the law protects an Englishwoman's property. Now let us see what protection it affords to her person. A wife is regarded by the law as part of the husband's goods and chattels; and, in olden times, women were absolutely sold by their fathers to the husband. Even in these days there are some (of course very ignorant persons) who believe that the law sanctions such a proceeding. Only the other day I saw a case in the newspapers of a man who sold his wife to another man for half-a-crown. Again how many cases of the brutal personal violence of men towards their wives, may be read of every day in the columns of our newspapers, and the very inadequate punishment frequently accorded to them, by the magistrates, for the offence. Many a man, I really believe, conscientiously holds with the old proverb:

> A wife, a dog, and a walnut tree,
>
> The more you beat 'em the better they be.

Again, if a woman is cruelly treated by her husband, she cannot leave him, or, if she does so, she can be compelled to return to him by law or by physical force. It is only legal separation by a court of justice, which can entitle her to live apart from him; and this legal separation is most difficult to obtain, and is only granted in cases of desertion and extreme cruelty.

Now what is the power of a woman over her own children, who are, at least, as much hers as her husband's? They are by law his children. He only has legal power over them; she can only act towards them by delegation from him; after he is dead she is not their legal guardian, unless he by will has made her so; he could constitute any stranger their legal guardian, and deprive their own mother of any power whatever over them. After seven years of age, the custody of a woman's children belongs exclusively to her husband; after that age she has not the right even to see them, unless by special legal decree.

'My brethren, these things ought not so to be!' But there are laws affecting both married and unmarried women, worse even than these; more degrading, more cruel, more unjust, more barbarous; laws, which if Englishmen once thoroughly understood, and reflected upon, would not, I venture to say, disgrace much longer the statute books of our country. And if women had the power of showing by their votes at an election, that they approved or disapproved of laws, which have so much to do with the happiness and well-being of their whole lives – if they had this power, would they not, I ask you, do their share in helping to abolish such legislation as this?

It is constantly said that women's interest are so carefully guarded by men that it is unnecessary to give them any voice in the matter. Did working men think that their well-being was so completely safe in the hands of the richer classes, that it was unnecessary to pass the representation of the People's Bill? We women demand, as men have demanded before us, the right to protect ourselves; and we believe, as they believed, that this end will only be gained by our obtaining a voice in the framing of those laws which we are called upon to obey.

At the commencement of my lecture I expressed a hope that before I had finished speaking I might have convinced some of those who differed from me on this subject, that politics have, after all, a great deal to do with women; that as they cannot live in the world without bearing a part in its business, responsibilities, and sufferings, they therefore do well to strive for a share of the power to work with men, for the general well-being and prosperity of their common country. In order to do this, I have pointed out, that they demand the removal of their electoral disabilities, believing that until this is done they can have no efficient weapon with which to fight their battles. We are constantly told, in tones of scorn, that the women who desire the suffrage are a mere handful of female fanatics. As compared with the entire female population we may be only a handful, but we are an ever-increasing handful of very obstinate people; and, if a wilful man must have his way, a wilful woman is likely to be quite as invincible:

> If she will, she will, you may depend on't;
>
> And if she won't, she won't, and there's an end on't

Every year a larger number of petitions are presented to Parliament in favour of this measure, and last year these petitions were signed by 187,000 persons. One hundred and eighty-seven thousand persons is, at any rate, a considerable handful, especially if they are all, as they have declared to be, violent fanatics.

Before I conclude I must make it clearly understood what the measure really is to which you will be asked to assent in the Resolution which will be put to this meeting. There is apt to arise a little obscurity on this point, I know. At a meeting in one of the large towns in the North, a short time ago, the Mayor, who was to preside, came up to me just before the meeting began, and said, in an excited manner, 'Now promise me that you will not advocate suffrage for married women'. I have no doubt that my worthy chairman had visions of his wife rushing to the polling-booth to record her vote in favour of the wrong candidate; and, worse still, of being kept waiting for his dinner! However, I assured him, as I now assure you, that we are seeking in any way to change the present basis of the suffrage. We only ask that women fulfil the same conditions as men – who are householders, who pay taxes, and are rated to the relief of the poor, shall be admitted to the franchise. More than this we do not ask – at present.

I have not attempted, this evening, to answer many of the objections that are commonly urged against giving women the suffrage. So much has already been said and written on the subject that those who wish to read the arguments on either side can easily obtain pamphlets by application to the secretaries of the Association.

In conclusion I will quote from one, whose name in the cause of freedom is of world-wide fame, and whose words, taken in their widest meaning, will need no comment of mine. What he – a man – pleaded for men, I – a woman – would plead for women. Mr John Bright, in upholding the claims of working men to the suffrage, said: 'England has long been famous for the enjoyment of personal freedom by her people. They are free to think, they are free to speak, they are free to write; and England has been famed of late years, and is famed now the world over, for the freedom of her industry, and the freedom of her commerce. I want to know, then, why it is that her people are not free to vote? Who is there that will meet me on this platform, or will stand upon any platform, and will dare to say, in the hearing of an open meeting of his countrymen, that these millions for whom I am now pleading, are too degraded, too vicious, and too destructive to be entrusted with the elective franchise? I, at least, will never thus slander my countrymen. I claim for them the right of admission, through their representatives, into the most ancient and most venerable Parliament which exists among men; and when they are admitted, and not till then, it may be truly said that England, the august mother of free nations, herself is free!' (Garrett, 1872.)

As you can see from the above speech, Rhoda was a most eloquent speaker and she had now become a prominent speaker on women's suffrage! Such was her fame that photographic portraits of her and some of the other prominent speakers were available at 1 shilling each. One such advertisement in *The Examiner* on 24th August 1872 stated:

'Women's Suffrage

Excellent Photographic Portraits of Miss Lilias Ashworth, Mrs Fawcett, Miss Rhoda Garrett, Mrs Rose, and other ladies in this movement, will be forwarded post free on application with stamps, or P.O. Order, to Mr Croucher, at Messrs Dando, Hulson, and Co's. Publishers, 151 Strand, W.C., or Winkfield-road, Wood-green, London, at 1s. each, or six for 5s…'

Unfortunately, I have not yet been able to find one of these portraits of Rhoda.

Chapter 9
The Taunton Election

During the nineteenth century, there were only two political parties, the Conservatives and the Liberals. The Labour Party wasn't formed until 1900. Since December 1868, The Right Honourable William Gladstone (Liberal Party) had been Prime Minister with The Right Honourable Benjamin Disraeli (Conservative Party) being the leader of the opposition.

During the period of this government's tenure, there had been 38 by-elections from 1868-1873 up to the date of the Taunton By-Election. Of these, the Conservatives had won 30 of these.

This election was one of the first following the 1872 Ballot Act, which had been introduced to attempt to stop the bribery, corruption and intimidation at elections by holding a secret ballot. However, the practices did not stop until the Corrupt and Illegal Practices Act of 1883, which stated what a candidate could spend their money on.

Fig. 26 Sketches from the Taunton Election showing the secret ballot in operation.

The by-election was called because the standing MP, Mr Henry James (Liberal), had been conferred the distinguished honour of becoming the Solicitor General and needed to seek re-election. His opponent was Sir Alfred Slade standing for the Conservatives.

Any by-election during this period was attracting the attention of the Women's Rights Movement. So, Rhoda Garrett travelled to Taunton for this election along with Lilias Ashworth to further their campaign. All they were trying to advocate and carry here was a bill which, as far as women were concerned, would assimilate the parliamentary with the municipal franchise, so that a single woman having a household or property qualification should be entitled to vote for the return of Members of Parliament. Benjamin Disraeli had already given his assent to the demand in the spring of 1873 and Sir Alfred Slade was perfectly ready to endorse the view of his leader. However, Mr James had made his best speech in the House against the bill presented by Mr Jacob Bright embodying this object. So, Rhoda and her friends bore him, politically, no good will.

In the days preceding the election, Sir Alfred Slade spoke most nights from the balcony of the Castle Hotel in front of crowds numbering five to twelve hundred people. Mr James was staying at the London Hotel, which also had a balcony but he preferred not to use it, he instead had several private meetings.

Rhoda was anxious to explain, in a few words, from the balcony of the Castle Hotel, what it was she really was asking for and to explain why she and her friends intended to canvass for Sir Alfred Slade. However, etiquette dictated that a stranger to the town could not speak from the balcony supported by the Conservative leaders. The special correspondent wrote in his article for the *London Evening Standard* on 4th October 1873, that 'I sincerely trust she [Rhoda Garrett] will yet have the opportunity given her, since I think it only right to add that Miss Garrett and Miss Ashworth unite with that charm of manner which it is the privilege of their sex, a moderation and temperance of speech, an earnest but thoroughly tranquil zeal, which it is impossible not to admire. They may not convert every one with whom they converse; but no man could converse with them once and ever ridicule either them or their cause again. They have both the manner and the mind which command respect.'

Just before the day of the election, Mr James did, however, appear on the balcony under curious circumstances, which showed the state of feelings held in the town and of the way both sides conducted the election. Sir Alfred Slade was to speak from the balcony of the Castle Hotel as usual at 8.15pm. There were already 600-700 people in the street around the market place and the windows opposite were thrown open, the rooms being mostly occupied by ladies, including Rhoda Garrett and Lilias Ashworth. He had that evening intended to explain to what extent he agreed with Rhoda and the campaign. The special correspondent witnessed and wrote what happened next during Sir Alfred Slade's speech as follows:

'Surrounded by all the leading Conservatives of Taunton, who stood on the balcony behind him, he was making a capital speech on the Ballot Bill. Suddenly a detonation was heard on the market place, and the crowd slowly received an unwonted accession of strength. Fresh people poured in from various quarters, and the cheering seemed to increase. On the balcony, however, it was soon observed that the cheering did not stop. Suddenly, on the opposite side of the street, a window in an unlighted house was thrown up ostentatiously, and with a clatter, and Mr James appeared outside it. Another detonation was heard from the market place; the crowd was swelled by yet fresh comers, and such a roar of voices was heard as I for one never heard before. It was now plain that, maddened by the success of the Conservative candidate, and by the speeches of himself and his friends, the Liberals had determined they should be heard no more. Sir Alfred held his ground, and said nothing: it would be vain to do so. Some twelve to fifteen hundred people were cheering and shouting against each other, and the sound was of the buzz of bees in a hive multiplied a million-fold. This went on for about twenty minutes, Mr James looking on the while. At last the Conservatives below could stand it no longer, and by main force they ejected the intruders. Mr James apparently took the hint, for he retired. Sir Alfred, much fatigued by the labours of the day, finished a first-rate speech triumphantly, but somewhat briefly. Then at his request, Mr Alfred Austin came forward, and at once launched a rapidly-delivered denunciation of one who, he said, after having been a quarter of a century at the bar, ought to be able to meet argument, and even ridicule, with some happier rejoinder than the roaring of the less responsible portion of his supporters.' (*London Evening Standard*, 1873.)

Mr James did send a letter of apology the next day expressing his regret for his supporters and repudiated any share in causing it and overall, he appears to have conducted the election with fairly good humour and temper. The apology was accepted by Sir Alfred Slade.

Also, prior to the ballot, Mr James talked about women's suffrage, stating 'that ladies referring to Miss Rhoda Garrett and Miss Caroline Biggs – day by day were frequenting the houses of electors in Taunton and telling the wives that they did not have their fair rights and privileges; that they, in their position with their husbands, were mere slaves, and that the law ought to be altered to give them greater freedom. If that were the case, wives would have found it out for themselves; and there were no greater traitors against the domestic happiness alike of men and women than those ladies, who generally being social failures, endeavoured to become political successes.' He then declared emphatically that if he lost his seat for Taunton ten times over, in the present state of feeling of women upon the subject, he was not going to support female suffrage, because he would know that he was acting in accordance with the sympathies and feelings of the country. He said this with a full knowledge of the consequence, that these lady agitators would silently dog his footsteps and oppose him at every election. (*Morning Post*, 1873.) These comments and others were also reported in *The Observer* and *The Times*.

Mr James, QC went on to win the by-election of Monday 13th October 1873, polling 899 votes to Sir Alfred Slade's 812. The declaration was received with rapturous cheering from the Liberals and with groans, hooting and cries of 'bribery' by the Conservatives.

A couple of days later it was reported that between 2.30pm and 4pm that votes were being offered at prices varying from a pound to half-a-crown. Which underlined the need for the Corrupt and Illegal Practices Act of 1883.

In the *South Wales Daily News* on Thursday 16th October 1873, the paper stated that 'Miss Rhoda Garrett writes to *The Times* with reference to a statement made the other day at Taunton by Mr Henry James that, "the ladies who had come into the borough to advocate the cause of women's suffrage went day by day into houses while men were absent and told their wives they had not got their fair rights and privileges – that in their position as wives they were mere slaves." Miss Garrett says: "In making this accusation Mr James must have been misinformed, as neither I nor the ladies referred to acted in the manner attributed to us by Mr James."' (*South Wales Daily News*, 1873.)

In another part of the letter she fears they cannot boast of having discovered a novel mode of electioneering, as affirmed by *The Observer*, as they only pursued the ordinary policy of any candidate to Parliament inimical to the views it advocates.

Mr Alfred Austin, a Conservative who had appeared alongside Sir Alfred Slade, wrote a letter to the editor of *The London Evening Standard*, which was published on Wednesday 15th October 1873 under the title "The Plain Truth about Taunton". The latter part of the letter reflected on Rhoda Garrett and her friends where he stated: 'I cannot, however, leave unnoticed the observations which are attributed to him [Mr James] by *The Observer*, and which have been reproduced by *The Times*, concerning Miss Rhoda Garrett and her friends. I sincerely trust the new Solicitor General did not employ the words imputed to him, for I can conceive none better calculated to injure him with men of fine taste. The ladies whom he represented to have described in such unmanly and infelicitous language are urging upon the attention of the public nothing more than has already received the oral support, and, in most instances, the vote in the House of Commons, of such men as Mr Gladstone, Mr Disraeli, Sir John Duke Coleridge - once a Solicitor General - Sir John Pakington, Sir Stafford Northcote, and that prince of sensible men, Mr Henley. I do not wish anyone to bow even to their opinion; but I think we may presume that a proposal which receives their countenance is nothing more than the assimilation of the municipal and parliamentary franchise as far as female householders and ratepayers are concerned. The assertion that there is the slightest wish, to excite married women against their husbands, must be pronounced either an ignorant or an impudent invention; and the endeavour to traduce Miss Rhoda Garrett and her friends by associating them with the American female agitators mentioned by *The Observer* – which, I doubt not, sinned from ignorance – is the most unjust thing I have ever heard of. I cannot pretend to say with accuracy what such a bastard phrase as "social failures" may mean, but as I have heard attempts to interpret it, I will venture to affirm that no society exists which would not be made happier by the presence of the gentlewomen - one of whom is a sister-in-law of Mr Fawcett, MP [Author's note: Mr Fawcett was married to Millicent Garrett, a cousin of Rhoda's - so she was not his sister-in-law] who have been thus rudely traduced, and the privilege of having made whose acquaintance will ever remain my pleasantest memento of the Taunton election.' (*London Evening Standard*, 1873.)

Rhoda and other suffragists, as they were later to become known, tried to achieve change, as we have seen, by lobbying Members of Parliament sympathetic to their cause to raise the issue of women's suffrage in debate on the floor of the Houses of Parliament. These debates took place nearly every year between 1870 and 1884, which kept the issue in the public eye, especially as it was reported both in the national and regional press.

Millicent Fawcett said of her cousin in her book, *What I Remember*, that, 'She became a speaker of extraordinary power and eloquence. Many of her hearers declared her to be quite unequalled for her combination of humour with logic and closely reasoned argument. Sometimes the newspaper comments were very droll. One which sticks in my memory ran thus: "The Lecturer, who wore no hat, was youthful but composed, feminine but intelligent."' (Fawcett, 1924.)

Many newspapers, through their articles, would ridicule the cause and the women involved.

The following article in *The Ipswich Journal and Suffolk, Norfolk, Essex and Cambridgeshire Advertiser* on Saturday 3rd May 1873 best illustrates the views of Parliament and the Press at the time:

'The advocates of the extension of the Parliamentary suffrage to women have once more aired their opinions, in and out of Parliament. The Press is generally opposed to them, and all sorts of arguments against the proposed change have been called forth by the Parliamentary debate. It seems to be generally argued that if women be admitted to vote for Members of Parliament they must also be admitted to sit in Parliament. It is also held that it would be impossible to admit women who are "femmes sole" to a right to vote without admitting the principle that all women should have votes. It may be so; but, with reference to the first of these arguments, Miss Rhoda Garrett says that she does not care to sit in Parliament, and she very neatly parodied Cowper's verse "O Solitude where are the charms?" into "O Parliament where are thy charms?" &c., as a proof of the contempt which she feels for the House of Commons and its seats. But, we have previously pointed out, the arguments of Miss Garrett and her friends go straight for the enfranchisement of all women without any qualification whatever, and no doubt, when enfranchised, they would take every possible advantage of their position. We must look to the logical consequences of the act of enfranchisement rather than to the disclaimers – however wittily put – of isolated agitators. The real reason why women cannot be declared equal to men in their claims to civil and political rights is that they are not equal to men physically. They could not support or defend their claims by physical force on equal terms with men. It may be very shocking to many good people to say so, but the fact is, nevertheless, that the basis of all political power at the present moment is physical force. People are a little too squeamish in these days about admitting this, or the women who clamour for political power would be told more frequently that unless they can defend their position, if need be, by physical force their claims cannot be allowed.' (*The Ipswich Journal, and Suffolk, Norfolk, Essex and Cambridgeshire Advertiser*, 1873.)

It is very easy to see from the above article what Rhoda and her friends were up against.

Rhoda herself talked about the way the press handled past events in one of her speeches in 1875 when she recalled the following: 'I well remember when Florence Nightingale set out to the Crimea to nurse the sick and wounded in that terrible war; the opprobrium that was cast upon her motives, and the scorn that was expressed of her caring understanding,' and added that, 'they who praised, and many of those who cheered, the name of Florence Nightingale in 1875 would have been the first in 1854 to revile her, and to condemn a courageous originality which they could neither understand nor reconcile with their narrow and false ideas of womanly purity and modesty.' (*The Star*, Guernsey, 1875.)

At that same meeting in St George's Hall in London on 29th May 1875, following the defeat of yet another bill proposed by Mr Forsyth in the House, each of the principal speakers opposed to the Bill were answered by one lady.

The London Correspondent for *The Staffordshire Daily Sentinel* on Thursday 27th May 1875, a couple of days prior to the meeting, stated that: 'Mr Leatham is to be honoured by an answer from Mrs Fawcett, the ablest of all the female orators. Miss Lilias Ashworth will answer Mr Chaplin, and Miss Rhoda Garrett Sir Henry James. The ex-Attorney-General has already had experience of Miss Garrett's sharp tongue, and has rather winced under it. She was at Taunton during that memorable election of October, 1873, when he sought re-election, and having declared that the lady politicians were "social failures", stimulated them into an antagonism so severe that it was not far from bringing about his defeat. Miss Rhoda Garrett (who is cousin to Mrs Fawcett) is perhaps the most caustic, as Mrs Fawcett is the most calmly logical, of all the lady speakers…' (*The Staffordshire Daily Sentinel*, 1875.)

Examples of both types of journalism towards the subject I will now include, which demonstrate the point.

In the *North Devon Journal* on Thursday 17th December 1874, following a women's suffrage meeting, which had been held at the Hanover Square Rooms on 9th December, they wrote:

'The women's suffrage meeting at the Hanover Square Rooms on Wednesday night was very successful. The lady speakers were not only fluent, but cogent. Miss Rhoda Garrett is one of the most effective advocates whom the Association possesses. She has a quiet, sarcastic way of dealing with her antagonists, which, though rather galling to them, is exceedingly effective with the public. Miss Lydia Becker used an argument which has always seemed to me very powerful. It was this: A certain section of politicians are proposing to disestablish the Church, and will shortly make it a test question at the poll. Whether the step be right or wrong it is one in which women are deeply interested. I may add more especially interested, since to every two men who go to Church there are at least three women. Yet it is not proposed to consult women in the smallest degree upon this weighty question. That certainly does seem a very grave injustice.' (*North Devon Journal*, 1874.)

However, referring to the meeting held at St George's Hall on 29th May 1875, *The Western Times* reported on an article published in *The Daily Telegraph*, which *The Western Times* stated had Mrs Fawcett, Miss Becker, Miss Rhoda Garrett, Mrs McLaren, and other ladies, and the addresses are described as of a high order of eloquence. The remarkable bantering article in *The Daily Telegraph* went as follows:

'Many of the speakers used the old arguments that our present laws affecting their sex are not as judicious or as careful of the interests as they would be if there were women amongst the voters. These statutes affect the property of wives, divorce, the custody of infants, and wife-beating. We will not now undertake to explain or to defend our legislation under these headings; but who are the women they affect? Wives. Yet wives, according to Mr Forsyth's bill, are to have no votes. So that to redress the wrongs of women who have husbands we give political power to women who have not. This does not seem very logical. Miss Todd on Saturday denied that a husband could adequately represent the interests of the household or the wishes of his wife. "There is much belonging to the general life of women under a great variety of circumstances which is never likely to be understood," – until Mr Forsyth's bill is passed. This is news. It presents a rather odd picture. A wife will have no vote, therefore cannot make her feelings felt at the poll. Her husband cannot "understand" her; he is a man, and therefore not only stupid and coarse, but her natural enemy and the foe of her sex. To obtain sympathy and redress she therefore rushes to the enfranchised virgin in the next street. She will be her counsellor, consoler, and champion. Not dulled by domestic cares, or stifled in her aspirations by the "flattery" and "playful" treatment which Miss Rhoda Garrett, speaking for herself and her sisters [Author's note – should be cousins] on Saturday, so indignantly rejected and denounced, the unmarried voter will understand, by intuition we suppose, not only the wrongs of the wife but the right remedy. She knows the best system of law as regards her property. On the custody of infants she is a sage. The true way of arranging divorce is at her fingers' end. She can solve the wife-beating question at a glance. On the Contagious Diseases Act she can speak fearlessly for hours. She is not daunted by practical difficulties, or oppressed by facts; she launches theories with a courage that belongs especially to the invincible innocence and pure career of youth. We do not dare to differ from the exalted estimate of the modern maid. We would only say that the first converts to her capacity ought to be her married sisters. Somehow, wives, as a rule, are not in the habit of looking up to their unmarried female friends. Indeed, they have, on the contrary, a foolish habit of regarding marriage as a platform from which they can look down on all. Charles Lamb mentions how a bride of a few months received some remarks of his on cookery with open scorn. "What could an old bachelor know about it?" In "Middlemarch" the great-souled Dorothea is pitied by her sister happy in her home. "Since Celia's baby was born, she had had a new sense of mental solidity and calm wisdom. It seemed clear that where there was a baby things were right enough, and that error in general was a mere lack of that central poising force." We must now teach the Celia's – a rather numerous section – another way of regarding their Dorothea's; they must turn from their husbands, too dull to understand them, and entrust their rights, and the rights of "baby" himself, to the former objects of their pity – the unmarried women around. This apotheosis of maidenhood has novelty about it. The Greeks of old used to sacrifice a virgin to save the State; we must now sacrifice the State to the virgin.' (*Western Times*, 1875.)

Unfortunately, Rhoda, although she was not to see it in her lifetime, was proved right!

Chapter 10

House Decorators at No. 2 Gower Street

During 1874, Rhoda and Agnes set up their own business as house decorators. Rhoda for the last part of her training had been residing in a newly-built block of flats at 3 Cornwall Residences (Now called Cornwall Terrace Mews) between Baker Street Station and Regent's Park and Agnes moved from the Fawcetts' house in Vauxhall to live with her during the latter part of that year. It was from this flat that the firm "R & A Garrett" was formed. Cornwall Terrace Mews has now become a most sought-after place to reside.

Agnes and Rhoda had finally managed to succeed in their ambitions to become professionals in the field of architectural decorators. Just to think, only a few years earlier, they had had to overcome the prejudices of trying to follow the path they had so desired. If they had been boys and interested in architectural decorating then, they would have started apprenticeships at the age of about 15, but the cousins had begun their apprenticeships in 1871, when Rhoda was 30 and Agnes 26.

Moncure Conway in his autobiography had recalled meeting Agnes and Rhoda after their business had been established, and he wrote the following regarding them:

'...Agnes, and her cousin Rhoda Garrett, joined together to become house decorators. They were beautiful young ladies. They told me their adventures in trying to obtain training in their art. They went to the chief firm in London, whose manager was inclined to make fun of their proposal to become apprentices. Finding them skilful as designers, he said that if they were not women he could give them positions as subordinate directors in certain kinds of work. "But," he said, "young women couldn't get along with workmen. How could you swear at them? And think of nice ladies running up ladders!" One of them [this would have been Rhoda as this would have been typical of her sharp tongue] said, "As for swearing at the workmen, they would not need that if it were ladies who made requests; and as for the ladders, bring one here and see whether we can climb it or not!" The manager found some work for them, and in a year or two they opened their own establishment in Gower Street, and rose to success on the tide of enthusiasm for house decoration.' (Conway, 1904.)

In May 1875, with their fledgling business underway, the cousins moved in as the first tenants of Edward Clark who had been granted a new 21-year lease for No. 2 Gower Street on the corner of Bedford Square, Bloomsbury, with the rear entrance of the British Museum in close proximity. Gower Street then was closed to through traffic.

Just a few doors along at No. 8 Gower Street during the same period lived Edward Stanley Gibbons the stamp dealer and publisher.

Gower Street is now associated with the University College, London (UCL) and The Royal Academy of Dramatic Art (RADA), founded by Herbert Beerbohm Tree in 1904.

At the northern end of Gower Street was one of the first underground stations on the Metropolitan Railway, opened in 1863. The seven stations were Paddington (Bishop's Road) (now Paddington), Edgware Road, Baker Street (where Agnes and Rhoda had just moved from), Portland Road (now Great Portland Street), Gower Street (now Euston Square), King's Cross (now King's Cross St Pancras) and Farringdon Street (now Farringdon). The railway had been built to alleviate the traffic congestion in London with the huge number of carts, carriages and omnibuses.

Rhoda's cousin, Elizabeth, whose hospital was opened in 1890 (now the site of the Unison building) was located just along from Euston Square Underground Station.

One, if not the first, of their commissions was to decorate 4 Upper Berkeley Street, the home of Skelton and Elizabeth Garrett Anderson. They were to go on to successfully decorate many private houses.

So, what had they learnt in their apprenticeship and how would they apply this to their house decoration and what style were they advocating?

In answer to the above question, during their training Rhoda and Agnes had learnt a wide range of skills, including mixing of paints through to drawings to scale, design and even the laying of gas pipes. Therefore, they were quite capable of not only drawing the designs for their clients but also getting their hands dirty to complete the tasks in hand.

The country in this period was undergoing great political, social and economic change, seeing a rise in the wealth of the middle classes. The architectural and design styles were moving in three directions, namely: Aesthetic; Queen Anne; and the Arts and Crafts. These came about as a reaction to Gothic Art and all its excesses.

I believe the style they were advocating was the Arts and Crafts style, which formally began in 1867 as encouraged by William Morris.

Did Rhoda know William Morris personally?

Although in various books and other publications it is stated that there is no documentary evidence of an association, I am as sure as one can be that Rhoda certainly did.

The Society for the Protection of Ancient Buildings was founded by William Morris, Philip Webb and other notable members of the Pre-Raphaelite brotherhood with the inaugural meeting being held on March 22nd 1877 at Queen Square, Bloomsbury. The founding members of the society included two women, one of which was Rhoda Garrett! (The other incidentally was Anne Thackeray Ritchie.) So, the chances of her not knowing William Morris are negligible.

The founding members, including Rhoda, were deeply concerned with the way well-meaning architects were scraping away the historic fabric of too many buildings in their zealous "restorations". It was the proposed restoration of Tewkesbury Abbey by Sir Gilbert Scott which spurred William Morris into action to have the society formed.

Rhoda remained a member of the society until her death in 1882. She was also a member of the Royal Archaeological Institute. So, she would have been more than capable of conversing with William Morris and others.

The Arts and Crafts style seemed to focus on hand-crafted décor. This is best portrayed in the book, *Suggestions for House Decoration in Painting, Woodwork, and Furniture,* written and illustrated by Rhoda and Agnes Garrett, published by Macmillan in 1876; this book was the second to be published in the "Art at Home" series. The first having been written by the Rev WJ Loftie. The advertisement written by the Rev WJ Loftie at the beginning of Rhoda and Agnes's book stated: '…The so-called "Queen Anne" style, to the study of which the Miss Garretts have devoted their attention, is rather a selection and refinement of the beauties in form and colour of other styles than anything clearly distinct… Its best examples are found in our native red brick, and that for internal decoration it adopts both wood panelling and wall-paper, while comfort and convenience are said to carry beauty with them, and extraneous ornament is avoided, are facts which should recommend the style to our favourable consideration.' He goes on to add, 'Everyone who has a house of his own may, I hope, find useful hints for the rules of good taste apply to the cottage as well as to the manor house, and may be put into practice everywhere. Expensive decoration has not been advocated; nothing in fact, but what may be secured at the same cost as the ugliness which at present pervades too many even of our wealthiest homes.' (Garrett, 1877.)

Looking at the style of narrative used I believe the book would have been written by Rhoda. However, the illustrations could have been drawn by either Rhoda or Agnes as they were both exceptional artists.

So, why do I believe the narrative was written by Rhoda?

Firstly, the introduction especially shows her characteristic personality, which includes the way she "calls a spade a spade"! It is written as though she is talking directly to you.

Secondly, in a letter from Loftie to the publisher Alexander Macmillan on 11th March 1876 about the forthcoming book, provisionally titled *Home Decoration and Furniture*, he states that the book was to be 'an account of the more simple ways in which, without great expense, a home might be made pretty & also wholesome; with designs & illustrations of furniture the whole to consist of a kind of narrative, in which a house is described on which a great deal of money has been spent with a bad result, and the simple cheap way in which the same house may be made to look well. This was to be written by Miss Garrett [Rhoda], and was to contain her own experiences. She was to have £30 or £40 from Coates, but no arrangement has been made with her as to her English copyright. The book, which I understand, will very shortly be ready, was to be about 150pp – & the ms [manuscript] was to be accompanied with drawings done so that they could either be copied by photography on wood or zincographed.' (Crawford, 2002.)

I will now give a few extracts from the introduction, showing the style advocated and the way the manuscript has been written as follows:

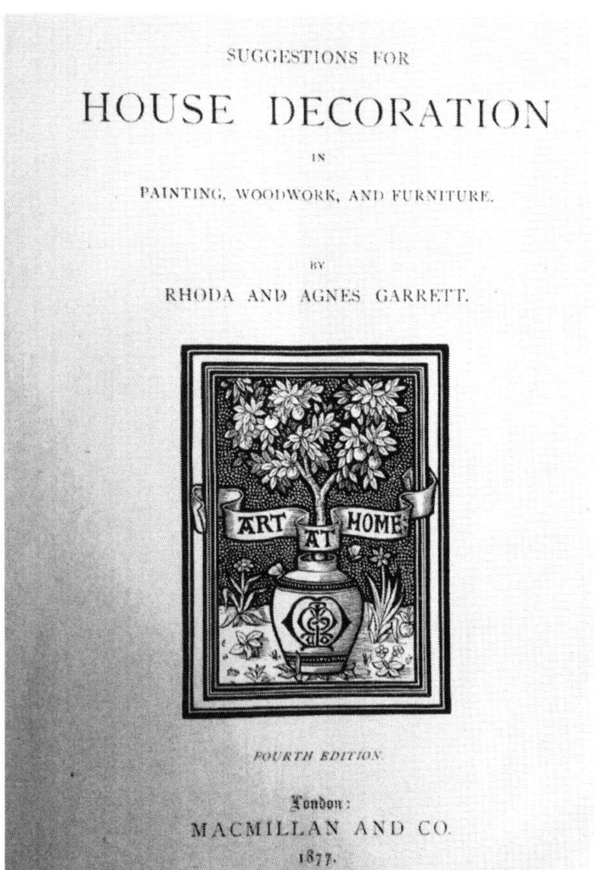

SUGGESTIONS FOR

HOUSE DECORATION

IN

PAINTING, WOODWORK, AND FURNITURE.

BY

RHODA AND AGNES GARRETT.

FOURTH EDITION.

London:

MACMILLAN AND CO.

1877.

Fig. 27

Insert page from the book that Rhoda and Agnes Garrett had published.

Firstly, comparing the Gothic revival and the Queen Anne revival she states, '...In order to discriminate justly between the merits of these rival styles, it is necessary not only to compare the cathedrals and wealthy houses of which each may boast, but to compare also the streets of either style and the small houses lying outside our cities. When this is done, the first thing discovered is that modern Gothic architecture seems to require stone. When a large house or a cathedral is to be built, this requirement will be no objection; money will be forthcoming and the building will be of stone. But if a builder is "running up a street of Gothic houses", what happens? It is out of the question that he should use as costly a material as stone, and stucco therefore takes its place. It is, we know, unreasonable to blame a pure and beautiful style for requiring a beautiful material; all we would urge is that for ordinary English houses, the style of house which was built during the eighteenth century, whose walls were of brick, and whose staircases were of wood (the houses, that is, which are now designated "Queen Anne"), are more suitable than the so-called Gothic house, with stone walls which are probably stucco, and with badly-constructed staircases of patent stone and iron, which in case of fire too often fall with their own weight. A better example of our meaning could not be given than a comparison between the houses in Bloomsbury – take Russell Square or Bedford Row – and the houses in South Kensington. These two districts were each built originally for the same class, and the comparison is therefore eminently fair, either for exterior or interior work. If we were fairies, the neatest way to make the comparison would be to change the position of a row of houses one night; and to transplant Bedford Row to Kensington. How the exterior of the houses would be admired! How relieved would paterfamilias be to find his lease relieved from that clause which obliged him to spend from £60 to £100 every third year in painting the whole façade of his house! And how equally pleasing would be his reflections on the solid fittings inside, the mahogany doors, the wooden wainscots that never chip, and the carefully constructed joinery of the window frames and sashes! In looking over such houses one is tempted to wish that as there is no chance of the transposition above alluded to, as the mountain cannot be taken to Mohammed, it were possible that at some time or other Mohammed might return to the mountain; in other words, that the fashionable world of London may one day return and live in the houses which were built in the solid and unpretentious style so much in accordance with the best characteristics of the English people.'

Secondly, she moves on to the interior fittings and decoration of houses and answering the objection of "Why do not house decorators create a Victorian style of decoration instead of going back to what they are pleased to call the Queen Anne style? Why is their cry still 'Backward Ho!?'" by saying: 'First a few words as to that misunderstood term "decorator". Until lately a house-decorator (to all except the extremely wealthy) has meant simply a man who hangs wallpaper and knows mechanically how to paint wood. In his proper place, he would fulfil the part which a dispenser does to a doctor, he should be able faithfully to follow directions, and honestly to carry out instructions; and as a rule, this role he is able to fulfil. But a decorator should mean someone who can do more than this; he should be able to design and arrange all the internal fittings of a house, the chimney-pieces, grates, and door-heads, as well as the wall-hangings, curtains, carpets, and furniture. All these it has hitherto been customary to entrust to different people, none of whom has had any part in the deliberations of the other. The consequence of such a disjointed arrangement has been that in modern houses one seldom finds a room which makes a harmonious whole.'

Finally, her personality shows through in this passage where she answers her own questions! '...Why has this old furniture survived so long? Is there any reason why woodwork should not be made now which shall last in the same manner as these old things have lasted? The answer to the first question is that these old pieces of furniture were designed and made by men (and often designed and made by the same man) who were thorough masters of their work and understood the construction of every part of it. Nowadays however, it is no uncommon thing for the designer of a piece of furniture to know little or nothing of its construction, so that cabinetmakers will say that architects bring them designs for furniture which are impossibilities when they are drawn out. It is the ordinary thing to lay all the blame of ill-constructed and badly-executed furniture upon the workman, but his (like many things in this life) is taking an unfair advantage of a worker who, on this topic at least, is seldom or never heard in his own defence. The designer, the workman, and the public are all blameworthy for any deterioration which has taken place in the construction of woodwork. Formerly a man who called himself a cabinetmaker and joiner had served an apprenticeship to every part of his trade. There were many traditions too which descended from father to son, a precious inheritance of which the value was scarcely appreciated until it was lost. Now we have changed all that; one man makes legs, another turns rails, a third makes framings, a fourth fits panels; and what is the consequence? Not one of these four men has ever troubled himself to enter into the spirit of the design; not one of them has felt the least interest in the piece; he has only cared to turn a leg or to fit the frame with as much expedition and with as little trouble to himself as possible.

The first thought which occurs to most people on finding such a system at work as this is, "But why do they do it so? Surely not from choice, for it must be dull work to go on day after day turning legs or making rails?" And to this we would make answer that the public themselves are mainly to blame. They demand cheap and showy furniture, and the only way to make furniture at once cheap and showy is to make it by machinery, and to turn men who make it as nearly as one can into machines; one is a rail-turning machine, another is a leg-making machine, and so on. It is as possible now as ever it was to get really good woodwork made, but it is, of course, more expensive than that made in the manner indicated above.' (Garrett, 1877.)

It is amazing that this was written over one hundred and forty odd years ago. However, the sentiments could still be said today! (Reproduction copies of their book are still available today for purchase.)

The book is divided into four chapters. Firstly, "Houses as They Are", split into sub-categories for the rooms described, namely, The Hall; The Dining Room; The Drawing Room; and The Bedrooms. It seems a shame that they didn't go on to cover The Kitchen. Secondly, "Houses as They Might Be", split into the same sub-categories. Thirdly, a chapter called "Draperies", which included a section on "Portieres and Chimney Piece Draperies", and finally a chapter on "What Will It Cost?".

Fig. 28 (above) View of drawing room.

Fig. 29 (right) Dressing table and glass.

Fig 30 (left)

Dining-room chimney piece.

Fig. 31 (right)

Drawing-room chimney piece (shows types of furniture at Standen House).

Fig. 32 (left)

Hall table and chair.

All the above illustrations are from 2 Gower Street that appear in Agnes and Rhoda's book.

Fig. 33 Rhoda about to give a speech.

Rhoda, on Tuesday 17th October 1876, read a paper at the annual meeting of the National Association for the Promotion of Social Science (NAPSS) in Liverpool, entitled *How to Improve the Interior of Modern Houses, with special reference to their Furniture and Decorations*. Incredibly she managed to have the largest attendance of any paper read at any of the meetings on any section at that year's conference between October 10th and 17th. The conference was split into five sections, namely: Jurisprudence and amendment of the law; Education; Health; Economy & Trade; and, for the first time, Art. The report following the conference in *Transactions of the NAPSS* describes Rhoda's paper as follows:

'Miss Garrett observed that the first step for carrying out any improvements in the house must be to devise some means of giving an appearance of better proportion to the rooms. It is easy to see that the height is out of proportion, and thus the area of the room is apparently reduced. The effect of bad proportion is further increased by the unbroken uniformity of the wall surfaces; there are not, as in the carefully planned rooms of an earlier period, any of those ancient recesses and corners, which, of themselves, suggested a pleasing picturesqueness in the treatment of rooms. When, as is generally the case, the rooms are thus too high, and the surfaces of the walls continuous and unvaried, the disagreeable effect can be in some degree modified: first, by dividing the wall by means of strings, cornices, or panels, and secondly, by a careful attention to the colouring of both walls and ceilings. It can easily be imagined that, if instead of covering the entire surface of the walls with an obtrusive paper of bad design and crude colour, some plan were adopted for dividing the height by means of wooden mouldings fixed to the wall so as to form either a dado or a deep frieze, the room would be brought into more graceful proportions. The divisions thus formed might be decorated in various ways, care being taken to get the deeper and heavier colour at the bottom of the room and the lighter towards the top. It is also a generally safe rule to avoid placing any elaborate pattern on a level with the eye, but to arrange the chief part of the ornament either above or below the middle compartment of the wall. The revival of plaster work for decorative purposes is much to be desired; but workmen are now so unaccustomed to the execution of designs involving more than the merest mechanical skill, that, for some time at least, the cost of carrying out such work would be considered by many at least out of proportion to its decorative value. It is to be hoped that some public-spirited householders will be found willing to sacrifice their purses to the general good, and submit their walls and ceilings to the "prentice hands of the artificers in this branch of the decorator's craft". With regard to the colouring of a room, there are many things to be taken into consideration before deciding upon the best tints to employ: for instance, the aspect of the rooms, and whether the light admitted by the windows will be light and warm or cold and sombre. In town houses this consideration is of the first importance, as the relative harmony of the colours will be changed by the quality of light in which they are seen. As a general rule bright colours should be used sparingly, and soft and delicate tints employed for the general tone of walls and woodwork. Whenever ornament is introduced for the decoration of the walls, it should be flat and unobtrusive, and the chief aim of the designer should be to make the predominating colour of the room an harmonious and suitable background for the picture, of which the walls are after all only the framework. In decorative painting, harmony is more desirable than contrast; but it will be found as a rule, that really good and carefully chosen colours seldom clash with each other if they are appropriately and judiciously placed. A great deal might be said about the fixtures in a room, such as chimney-pieces, doors, windows, and the like – for nothing makes more difference in the general effect of a room than appropriate and graceful designs in these particulars. In a climate like this, the chimney-piece (no longer the chimney-corner) must be the chief point of interest in the room for nine months out of every twelve, and thus it behoves us to make it worthy of the important position it occupies. The writer would not suggest that the faults of the old-fashioned fireplace should be reproduced, but the adaptation of its picturesque and ornamental features to modern requirements. Windows and doors may be much improved by skilful treatment; the proportion of doors may often be improved by the addition of some kind of pediment or other finish to relieve the square ugliness of the architecture; and windows can have screens of coloured and tinted glass, without returning to what has been called the "bottle-green period". In furnishing, the first thing that demands attention is the right appropriation of the furniture to the purpose for which it is required; and, as a general rule, it may be said that the style of the furniture ought to be suited to the main characteristics of the architecture of the building. The colours, textures, and uses of drapery are not properly appreciated and employed to the best advantage; and yet drapery is a simple and effective means of softening the hard lines and angles of walls and woodwork, and blending the details of the room into one harmonising whole.

In conclusion, Miss Garrett remarked that women's sphere and women's mission is one of the most important problems of the present day, but here, at least, in the decoration and beautifying of the house, no one will dispute their right to work. If women would rightly undertake this work, and would study to understand the principles upon which all art – decorative art as well as the higher branches of art – is based, they would not only thereby increase their own sources of happiness; but in thus extending the gracious influence of the home, they would help to raise the position of household art, and thus render a real service to the nation.' (Ryalls, 1877.)

As you can see from the last paragraph, Rhoda still managed to include a comment about women's suffrage.

Without going into further detail of their book, an idea of the sort of work carried out by Rhoda and Agnes was given by their great friend, the composer, Hubert Parry. He was working in insurance during the initial time that they knew him as an underwriter for Lloyd's of London. Hubert Parry was to marry Lady Maude Herbert in 1872 (she was a direct descendant of the Spencer/Churchill family to which the late Diana, Princess of Wales was also descended from. Lady Maude was also involved in the women's suffrage cause, attending many meetings.)

Hubert Parry stayed with Rhoda and Agnes at 2 Gower Street for a fortnight from 9th May 1876 and he remarked in his diary that, 'I was never so spoilt in my life. They seem to divine all one's wants before one has thought of them oneself. They are the best company I ever knew, and to live in their house is a very great deal of happiness in itself. The quiet and soothing colour of the walls and decoration and the admirable taste of all things acts upon the mind in the most comforting manner. I was quite excised of the vulgar idea that everything ought to be light & gaudy & covered with gilt in London. All these are a sure element of discomfort in a house, ones eye wants rest & nothing shows the dirt & dust of London so soon as light colours of gilding.'

It was regarding Hubert Parry's stay with Rhoda and Agnes over this fortnight that the only two letters I know of in existence, written by Rhoda Garrett on "R & A Garrett" headed writing paper to Lady Maude have survived. I have transcribed both letters that appear in the appendices below: (Letters from Rhoda Garrett to Lady Maude Parry, 1876.)

The first one dated 9th May 1876.

'My dear Lady Maude

Just a line today that Mr. Parry is coming to us this evening. We will take good care of him though I am sure he will be dreadfully bored without you. We telegraphed to him yesterday when we got his letter, to come up here at once: but he could not manage to come last night. Agnes was in despair when he did not turn up for dinner as, remembering some of his likes, she had got oysters & her housekeeperly mind was much disturbed! Before we knew Mr. Parry was coming we arranged to go to the "Prince of Wales" tonight to see "Ours" & we are afraid that will bore him horribly: but if he does not care to go with us we shall leave him at home with his pipe and everything else we can think of to pass the time. We liked your letter very much and were much amused with your account of things. We are angry too at you being shut in like a besieged city, but we had better hold our peace as we are apt to be violent when we think about it. "Whoso liveth his life shall lose it."

We are delighted to think you will go to Littlehampton where we know you will be taken care of & Dorothea will flourish in the Sussex milk. We shall see Mrs. Shepherd before you go down & if we can manage it we shall run down & see you while you are there.

Ever yours, with our love

R Garrett'

[Author's note: The play, *Ours*, was by TW Robertson and Miss Ellen Terry (later to become the leading Shakespearian actress in Britain and subsequently to be made a Dame) played the part of Blanche Haye in the revival of this play at the Prince of Wales Theatre. The theatre is not the same as the one in Leicester Square, which was built in 1884, but the "Scala Theatre" which was called the "Prince of Wales" between the years 1865-1882. It used to be on Charlotte Street, off Tottenham Court Road. (Just a few minutes' walk from their house in Gower Street.) The theatre was demolished in 1969, after it had been destroyed by fire.]

The second letter was dated 19th May 1876.

'Dear Lady Maude

We have had a grand fight with Mr. Parry this morning because he declared his intention of going to Harley Place for no reason that we could make out except that "it was good for him to be uncomfortable".

We have conquered however, after a severe conflict & now he will remain here now like an orderly Christian. We shall take him to church tomorrow & see that he says his prayers reg'lar. So you need not be uncomfortable about his spiritual welfare. Agnes & he have just gone out to see if they can meet with a decent piano for him to use while he is here. Also we hope he will give us the pleasure of hearing him play. We tell him it will benefit our souls. We are getting very sordid with the too constant pursuits of gold! The soiree was quite a success. We wished you had been there. Many times during the evening and many of our friends asked after you and regretted your absence to the cause. I hear you are getting thin in a very improper manner, do you take lots of milk? That's what I live on when I can't eat. We <u>must</u> have you strong bodied, as well as strong minded! This horrible weather & keeps everybody that is not strong from getting well: The east wind gives me a constant cold. We took Mr. Parry to dine at the Albemarle Club last night, he wants you to belong to it. When you get back to London you must come with us there to see what you think of it. Little Philippa (wor? O! wor?) was here on Thursday & was particularly interested in seeing "Dorothea's Papa". She is exceedingly curious about that young lady & wanted to know if she was short-coated yet? Our love – (We wish you were here too)

Ever yours,

Rhoda Garrett.'

[Author's note: Little Philippa was Henry and Millicent Fawcett's child; she was 8-years old when this letter was written, and Dorothea was Hubert and Lady Maude's first child, known later as Dolly; she was just 4-months old. The Albemarle Club was a private members club which opened in 1874 and was open to both men and women. The club came into criticism because of its progressive views on women's rights.]

Most of the alterations made to 2 Gower Street, as can be seen in the illustrations in their book, were made prior to Rhoda's death in 1882. Moncure Conway tells how, 'Some friend, calling upon them, reported that, though the interview was interesting, the ladies could not be seen, as they were up on a scaffolding, lying flat on their backs close to a ceiling which they were painting.' (Conway, 1882.)

One of the ceilings mentioned above on the first floor was in the drawing room and the other was their office in the room behind. The latter survives in situ conserved by the University of London and the former, which was too unstable to remain in place, is now held in sections by the University of London Archive. The one which was in the drawing room was coloured pale green, pink and yellow, featuring humming birds and flowers such as lilies, passion flowers, tight rose buds, periwinkles and red primroses. In the four corners of the ceiling were portraits of Michelangelo, Rubens, Raphael and Titian. Whereas the smaller back room of similar colours had portraits of poets including Keats and Shakespeare.

Although Hubert Parry had a preference and liking for Rhoda and Agnes's Gower Street property, he was unable to persuade his wife in preferring a property in Bloomsbury over the showy exteriors of Kensington. The Parrys were to take a property in Lower Phillimore Place, Kensington later in 1876. Hubert's first action on having his offer on the house accepted was to invite Rhoda round. R & A Garrett were given the commission of redecorating the house to make it habitable.

It is fortunate that Sir Hubert Parry and Lady Maude's along with their eldest daughter's diaries have been kept by the Ponsonby family at Shulbrede Priory as it is from Sir Hubert Parry's diary that can be found glimpses of the Garrett cousins at work on a commission.

Some of the entries show that not everything went as smoothly as he would have wished on the commission and the following entries in November 1876 give a glimpse of this as follows:

'9 Nov. Went down to the new house in the morning & waited there several hours for the Garretts who never came.'

'10 Nov. To the house in the morning when came Rhoda to settle about carpets & such like...'

'13 Nov. Got up to town cold & not a little chilled & found the house almost uninhabitable. Not a single carpet down of course, but most of the rooms also blocked by fresh paint all round the borders, & the furniture & property generally piled in great heaps in the middle. Not a table clear, no bed to sleep in, nothing to eat, & only one fire alight in the room where the workmen were painting.'

'15 Nov. A carpenter and a carpet man & woman arrived early & got to work to put things in their places – & shortly after Rhoda – who took off her great coat & said, "I have come to work" & work she did. First fetching a charwoman to help our servants & then setting to dust & arrange everything & directing everybody else what to do; progress was made with quite marvellous rapidity so that by the time Maude arrived in the

afternoon the house in some parts looked positively comfortable... meanwhile Agnes arrived & the house was put more & more into order & then having given further directions the two devoted Garretts departed to find a cook for us. Which they did after great trouble & telegraphed to that effect & the cook arrived next morning.'

About a year later, Rhoda showed that she didn't mind getting involved in the nastier side of architectural decoration when a problem was found in the drainage system. Parry noted in his diary in October 1877 the following entry on the cook's discovery of a bad drain, saying, 'I went to the scullery to see, & found a tremendous stink and the man taking an accumulated mass of filth some 18 inches deep which was part of an accumulated refuse of many years. He [Dodd, the cook] said he thought it a very bad state of things, & wanted me to go and fetch one of the Miss Garretts to see it. I went off to fetch one of the Garretts. I found them at home & they immediately telegraphed for the head builder to meet them at Phillimore Place in the afternoon. I stopped to luncheon & then Rhoda came back with me... after consultation with Rhoda they concluded that the whole drain system must be entirely reconstructed, at present it absolutely poisons breathing through every vent hole in the house; it will take quite a fortnight to do & cost a large sum of money.'

Unfortunately, little evidence of Rhoda and Agnes's house designs are available to be viewed today. However, furniture they designed for James and Margaret Beale's move from 41 Gordon Square, Bloomsbury to 32 Holland Park in London (one of the first commissions outside the family they had received) were later moved to Standen House, their Sussex home (now owned by the National Trust). This country house was built by Philip Webb (architect) who was a close friend of Rhoda and Agnes and decorated by William Morris & Co. The pieces of furniture that have survived are a daybed; corner cabinet; chair; bookcase; settee; footstall; and a hall cupboard inscribed with the Beale's initials and the year 1875. This latter piece of furniture is still owned by one of their descendants. Both the daybed and the corner cabinet can be seen in the decorated rooms of 2 Gower Street as shown in the Garretts' book.

Some of these pieces currently on show at Standen House are pictured in Figs. 34-37 opposite.

Fig. 34 (above) Dressing-room table.

Fig. 35 (right) Corner cabinet.

Fig. 36 (below) Chair.

Fig. 37 (above) Daybed.

More than one piece of each design appears to have been made, as, for example, the daybed was included at both the Paris Exhibition in 1878 and ten years later at an Arts and Crafts exhibition. In the Paris Exhibition, The Garretts' exhibit, set out as a bedroom, received the personal compliments of HRH the Prince of Wales, who was anxious to know the names of the exhibitors.

In March 1879, Rhoda and Agnes opened a showroom/warehouse, not far from their Gower Street home, at 4 Morwell Street. This was in the heart of London's furniture-selling quarter. Their business must have generated enough work as Agnes continued to pay rent and rates for this building until mid-1900, long after Rhoda's death.

The business had progressed well enough for them to be willing to take on their own apprentices at a premium of £300 lasting for at least three years. The apprentices would have to be prepared to work hard, having daily hours between 10am and 4pm. I doubt if Rhoda suffered fools gladly, as she wrote in a letter to *The Times* on 15th November 1878 that, 'Every woman who is working independently and has attained any measure of success knows what it is to have daily applications for employment which she cannot satisfy because the women who make them have no marketable commodity to offer, and are totally untrained to undertake any kind of skilled labour.'

A measure of the success of the cousins was eloquently portrayed in *The Dundee Chronicle*, on 21st March 1882, entitled "Rhoda and Agnes Garrett", saying, 'In an account of these two young ladies, the latter a sister and the former a cousin of Mrs Fawcett, we are told that they have achieved a remarkable success in their business as house decorators. Both are most refined in face and manner, pleasant of voice, bright in conversation, with that repose which the better class of Englishwomen always possess, very genial and evidently happy in their work. They are artists, but do not wear the swaddling-clothes of aestheticism, slight in physique, understand fully their business, are intelligent upon all topics of the day, and blessed with practical common-sense. They have taken a few lady apprentices for three years at a premium of £100 per annum; but they are too busy to take any one who has not a definite purpose.' (*Dundee Courier*, 1882.)

Chapter 11

Rustington – A walk in time

There were three places in England that Rhoda Garrett was especially associated: the first being her birth place of Elton, Derbyshire; secondly, her working career in Gower Street, London; but undoubtedly her favourite of the three was the small village of Rustington in West Sussex where she was to rent a cottage with her cousin Agnes from 1879. It is for this reason that I will now describe in detail the village she loved so much.

Fig. 38

The view from "The Firs" looking east.

It was in Rustington that she could relax with her pet dogs and other animals, meet her friends, and spend time walking around the village and along the seafront. The climate and the clean air would have been most beneficial for her poor level of health that she had continually suffered throughout her life.

The cottage they rented was called "The Firs", a dairy farm in The Street just west of the Parish Church of St Peter and St Paul. The original building was medieval with extensive grounds and outbuildings. The cottage was altered extensively in 1610 with the new front at right angles to The Street; it consisted of a largish, though rather dark drawing room and a front hall and large old kitchen with a stone floor and an old pump. The cottage (which has also been called "Old Orchard") has been extended since Agnes and Rhoda lived there. It is now a Grade 2 listed building. However, much of the garden area they so loved (a place I visited for garden parties in my youth) has subsequently been sold in recent times to build additional housing.

Fig.39

The cottage rented by Rhoda and Agnes Garrett called "The Firs".

Fig. 40 Rhoda (left) and Agnes sitting in the garden of The Firs.

If Rhoda were still around today she would have seen little change in Elton or indeed to some extent in London, but Rustington has changed out of all recognition, although some of the houses along The Street where she lived are still in existence.

Comparing the populations of Elton, London and Rustington in 1871 and 2011, it is easy to see why. In Elton, the population has dropped from 519 in 1871 to about 400 in 2011; in London, the population has approximately doubled from 4 million to 8 million over the same period; whereas in Rustington the population has risen from around 360 residents in 1871 to over 13,000 in 2011! The village now has no fields or woodland areas and possesses just a minute amount of green space or recreational facilities.

So, what was Rustington like when Rhoda was here?

I will now describe the village through the eyes of Rhoda as she walks around the village with her cousin Agnes and her pet dogs with the aid of maps of the village (see appendices) from this period and a description from a friend of the family, Mrs Ethel Theresa Day (nee Stansfield) (1864-1942), one of the daughters of the popular vicar Mr Edmund Stansfield, who wrote an extensive account in 1936 entitled *Rustington in the old days – sixty years ago or more*. Rhoda and Agnes would have taken these walks on numerous occasions whilst they lived in the village. (*The West Sussex Gazette*, 1936.)

Rustington back in 1879 seemed to be a very happy peaceful village, with a world of romance and beauty, kindliness and neighbourly love shining through its everyday life.

We shall start at the focal point of the village, the Parish Church of St Peter and St Paul, just a minute's walk due east of "The Firs" and heading west down The Street.

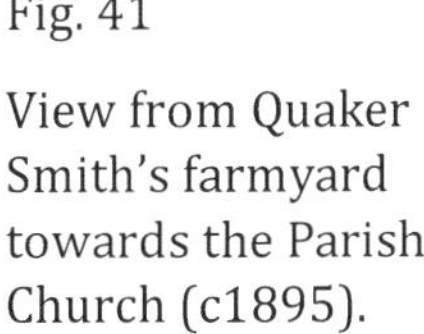

Fig. 41

View from Quaker Smith's farmyard towards the Parish Church (c1895).

Firstly, just over the road on the north side of the church was one of the six working farms in the village. This was Quaker Smith's farmyard. Rhoda and Agnes had noticed the fine, tall old man who was clad in the correct dim-hued cloth and wide hat of the Quakers. The farmyard looked richly prosperous, with its huge stacks of corn, hay and clover, with its splendid stables, haylofts and barns, which stretched as far as the Old Manor House. In the barns, the men would be threshing the corn with flails. The corn was all cut with reaphooks, so there was a good deal of wheat lying about. The women and children all went gleaning the corn in the long holidays, when they reckoned to pick up sufficient wheat to keep them in flour all the winter.

Next, on the north side of the road heading west, is the Manor House, which had a letter box outside on the edge of the road, which Agnes and Rhoda used to post their letters to London and elsewhere. The Manor House was mentioned in the Domesday Book. Here there was a magnificent barn, a large cart-shed and a pond. There were hugely thick walls that went along as far as the footpath running north up to Rustington House. (This is where Old Manor Road is now situated.)

Fig. 42

The front of the Manor House.

Fig. 43

The pond at the back of the Manor House.

Directly opposite the Manor House on the south side of the road was a little, long, low, cobbler's shop with a lattice window. Next to the cobbler's shop was The Lamb Inn (a single-storey building) and where the car park now is there was a charming old cottage called Rose Cottage, followed by Jessamine Cottage. Then there were some farm buildings before arriving at The Vinery, which has changed little since. We then pass the Garrett household before coming to Firs Cottage, which was the last of the cottages before one of the many wells in the village that the villagers used to draw up pails of water.

Fig. 44

Pound Cottage is on the left and Firs Cottage is on the right. The Firs can be seen at a right angle to the road.

On the north side of the road there are other properties, which still exist to the west of what is now Old Manor Road. The first of these was a large property called The Elms, followed by Tithe Barn and Pound Cottage, the latter being the village pound for stray cattle. Agnes rented Pound Cottage several years after the death of Rhoda.

Then, there was Mitchell's Cottage, Gardner's Cottage and Little Ffynches, which was once a sweet old cottage with a farmyard at the side and back of it. This property has always been a favourite for painters and for postcards. The last of the houses on the north side was Ffynches Lodge, which the Reverend Stansfield had built for his family for when he finished his ministry. The first tenants of this property were Mr Gerald Edward Wellesley, his wife Ada Hamilton Martin, and their children. Mr Wellesley was the great-nephew of the Duke of Wellington and was good friends of both Rhoda and Agnes. He would often tell stories of his great-uncle, including the unhappy marriage of the Iron Duke.

Fig. 45

A view, looking west along The Street with Little Ffynches on the right-hand side and Walnut Tree House on the left.

On the south side there were further cottages, including Granny Ball's Cottage and the larger Walnut Tree House and barns and finally Balchins Farm and cottages. Rents for these cottages in The Street ranged from one shilling to two shillings and sixpence a week.

Just past Balchins Cottage there was a Common Stile field where you had to climb over the high stile to take the short cut to Littlehampton (now Henry Avenue). There were no other houses as The Street then turned north into what is North Lane with large banks on either side. North Lane was a very narrow lane and here they would have noticed the wide grass borders and hedges rich with honeysuckle and dog roses and later with a harvest of blackberries and sloes. This walk would have been pretty and peaceful all the way up to the guide post at the junction with Worthing Road. From here you could travel west past Boundary Cottages on the border with Littlehampton towards Arundel and east towards Angmering and Worthing.

Along this stretch of the Worthing Road, travelling east, not far from the guide post was Rustington House, owned by the Squire, Mr Hugh Penfold. Again, there were no further houses east until you came to the next guide post by a splendid old mill and the Windmill Inn and one of the many ponds in the village.

We'll now return to the church and head east. On the north side, just past Quaker Smith's farmyard there was a footpath leading from the church north-east all the way up to the mill as previously mentioned. Opposite the Old School House and the Vicarage, where Woodlands Avenue now is, were deep ditches, the banks of which were a mass of white violets and a great meadow, with hedges and elm trees at intervals. Just beneath one of the huge elm trees was a heavy wide stile –

which the Garretts and others found very comfortable to sit on and watch the great old cart-horses on Sundays standing by the stile in the shade of the elm tree, swishing the flies from their bodies with their long tails.

Fig. 46

The old mill with The Windmill Inn on the right-hand side.

No cottages existed between the Vicarage and the guide post at the junction with Ash Lane and Broadmark Lane except that on the right-hand side just before the junction was the blacksmith's flint-built forge, later to become a chapel. It is difficult to believe that this street is where the shopping centre now is!

Fig. 47

The chapel, once the old blacksmith's shop.

On winter evenings boys would run to warm themselves, at the forge, on their way home from school; the blacksmith would never allow girls in his forge, though he would condescend to make them hooks with which to trundle their hoops.

At the junction, going south, was Broadmark Lane with Marters Cottage standing not far from the blacksmith's forge. That lane was particularly beautiful with its high hedges a mass of blossom in summer. There were a couple of cottages along Broadmark Lane called Bumble Cottage and Hedgerville before arriving at Broadmark Farm.

Going north from the guide post, in Ash Lane, there were two adjoined cottages, The Mathews and Stonefield Cottage followed by a brick yard and cottage before coming to Woodbine Corner with yet another guide post. North would take you up to The Mill and the Windmill Inn again, but due east the road continues past Palm Cottage. There were farms and cottages along this stretch including Pigeon House Farm (built in 1480), which is reputedly haunted, and West Preston Manor, which had an inn opposite called "The New Inn". The road then bends north past East Preston Church and up to Angmering Station before leaving the village.

Heading now back to the church.

Fig. 48

From this shop Mary Ann Humphrey made the "Rustington Buszard".

The village post office was right opposite the lych-gate entrance to the churchyard in Sea Lane with another pond to the left (south of the post office). It was not only a post office in Rhoda's time, but also a bakery, and a shop full of every requirement, from crockery to ham and sweets.

Old Mrs Humphrey, who ran the post office, was brought up on Cudlow Farm just down Sea Lane. Her cakes were quite celebrated, it was said that the spicy atmosphere of that little shop was most invigorating, where the perfume of bacon, cheese and candles met the fragrance of the newly-baked bread as it came floating in from the bake house beyond. However, it was her renowned lardy cake that was Rhoda and Agnes's particular favourite. The cousins always made a point of taking at least one back to London with them. Rhoda and Agnes thought the quality of the lardy cake was so good they renamed it "The Rustington Buszard" after Messrs Buszard, the celebrated cake makers in the West End of Oxford Street in London to whom they were very aware.

Fig. 49

A pot lid from Messrs. W & G Buszard in Oxford Street.

The recipe that Mrs Humphrey used would have been similar to the traditional Sussex Lardy Johns, but it is believed that she also added another ingredient to spice it up. The recipe is as follows:

<u>The Rustington Buszard</u>

¼ lb flour
2 oz. lard
¾ teaspoonful of baking powder
2 teaspoonfuls of sugar
Sprinkling of sultanas and/or currants

Quantities could be adjusted proportionately depending on the size required.

Method: Rub all the ingredients together in your hands and then add enough water to make a stiff paste. Once you have the stiff paste you can cut the paste into squares and bake for 10-15 minutes. (Samuelson, 1937.)

Unfortunately, unlike the Winster Wakes, the Rustington Buszard is no longer made in the village. Perhaps this could be the impetus to start a come-back!

Walking down Sea Lane from the lych-gate was The Grange, built in 1815; a little further down the same side of the road was Cudlow House and Farm. It was at Cudlow House that Rhoda and Agnes's great friends Hubert and Lady Maude Parry were renting from July 1878. It was in 1874 that the Parrys' acquaintance with the Garretts ripened into a friendship that never waned; Hubert Parry wrote in the latter part of 1874, stating that 'It is a real pleasure to spend time with such people, who discuss every point worth talking about with no personalities. Their whole conversation and everything about them rings true. But it makes one all the more bitter when one hears the false jargon of society again, and perhaps that's no harm either.'

In December 1874, Hubert Parry attended his first Woman's Rights meeting. In the first instance his interest in the movement may have been enlisted by his friendship for the Garretts. Miss Rhoda Garrett was one of the speakers and spoke very well according to Sir Hubert. However, his sympathies were genuine and survived his distaste for the militant tactics adopted in the second decade of the 20th century.

On 13th January 1876, Sir Hubert and Lady Maude Parry had their first daughter, christened Dorothea, after their favourite character in *Middlemarch*. However, Lady Maude, whilst staying at Wilton House, developed first diphtheria and then scarletina. The Parrys were in strict quarantine in Wilton for weeks. Once Lady Maude had been pronounced out of danger they moved back to London and the good services of Rhoda and Agnes continued, for it was they who recommended Littlehampton as a suitable place for rest and change, and were thus responsible for the long and happy association with Sussex, which lasted till the end of Hubert's life. Rhoda and Agnes had ordered their rooms at an "old-fashioned farmhousy kind of hotel near the beach", and they moved there on June 12th.

A few weeks earlier, Sir Hubert had recorded in his diary the following entries, detailing visits by Rhoda and Agnes:

Saturday May 18th: *'Day began with a thunderstorm & violent rain, but it cleared up after breakfast & continued beautifully fine & fresh. Had a bathe in the morning* [Hubert Parry was usually accompanied by Joe Olliver for bathing trips] *& a little walk in the afternoon. The Garretts made their appearance in the evening, after Maude had gone to bed.'*

Monday May 20th: *'...storms of rain on & off most of the day, however, I got a bathe in the morning & was the only bather. The Garretts came later, Maude not very well, feeling her tonsils again.'*

Sunday May 26th: *'I started for Littlehampton at 6*[p.m.] *– I arrived & found Maudie in the company of the Garretts, & apparently better in health and spirits.'*

Monday May 27th: *'Lovely day. Fresh light & clear. Had a bathe in the morning & then walked down the sands with Maudie & the Garretts & sat down in a comfortable sheltered corner by the mill & talked. Algologised...'* [Sir Hubert Parry also worked at marine zoology and algology whilst down the beach, looking for things to show his friends under his microscope.]

On one of their stays down in Littlehampton during 1878, Hubert Parry started house hunting in Rustington and wrote the following entry:

Monday June 24th: *'...In the afternoon Maudi & I drove down to Rustington, to see some houses which were to be let, one "The Grange" is quite an ideal snuggery, & would have done for me to perfection, but has been snapped up under our very noses.'*

The Grange had been rented by the Urlin family who became good friends with the Parrys and the Garretts. It was just a month later that Hubert and Lady Maude rented Cudlow House.

Cudlow House, as mentioned in the 1860s chapter, became associated with the story of "Peter Pan". JM Barrie was a frequent visitor to the property where the Llewellyn-Davies family lived with their dog, Smee.

The only other properties were on the same side as the post office, which were Boxtree Cottage and Hobbs Farm. Apart from a lane called The Wapple that went from opposite Cudlow House down to Mewsbrook House and Littlehampton it was all meadows. (Mewsbrook was then in Rustington, but later taken by Littlehampton when they moved the border.)

Fig. 50

Looking south along Sea Lane with Hobbs Farm on the right and Cudlow Cottages and on the left-hand side.

Fig. 51

Mewsbrook House, later to become The Towers Hotel.

Down at the bottom of Sea Lane was the beach where the rough road turned 90 degrees west towards Littlehampton. Just before the bend on the left-hand side stood another mill with cottages and, having travelled along the road parallel to the beach a short distance towards Littlehampton, was Seafield House.

Fig. 52

Mill and cottages at the bottom of Sea Lane. This was one of only two roads that went to Littlehampton from Rustington!

Fig. 53

The New Inn, which became Walnut Tree Cottage.

One other point of note walking around the village was that there were deep wide ditches on the sides of the lanes such as Broadmark Lane and Sea Lane. These would have aided the smugglers who could use them to travel with their booty unseen. Smuggling was rife along the Sussex coast right up to about 1820. Many of the houses in the village had holes to store the goods, including "The Firs", and there were reputably various underground passages used by the smugglers. The New Inn was the meeting place for the smuggling band "The Ragman Tots". They were so called as they used rags to disguise the noise of the carts as they moved though the village.

One of the many stories told by an old smuggler in the village to the Reverend Stansfield whilst Rhoda was in the village was of an occasion when the old smuggler said he had a fine run to escape the revenue officer, whilst carrying a keg of spirits. However, he had remembered that the table-top tomb near the church porch had a conveniently broken gap in it, into which welcome aperture he slipped his precious keg, and all was well.

Fig. 54

The Parish Church of St Peter and St Paul in Rustington.

Fig. 55

The interior of the Parish Church of St Peter and St Paul in Rustington with Reverend Edmund Stansfield.

Chapter 12
The Rustington Years

During 1878 and 1879, Rhoda and Agnes were very busy with their business, especially following the Paris Exhibition, which led to the renting of the warehouse/showroom in Morwell Street. Therefore, the renting of a property down in Rustington would have been a great way to have some rest and recuperation.

Sir Hubert Parry wrote a charming tribute to Rhoda and Agnes in a letter to Hugh Montgomery in the autumn of 1879 saying, 'We have got the Garretts in a little house in the village, and that it is as good as ever so much physic to Maud, as she is perfectly devoted to them, and they keep her in wonderfully good spirits.' (Graves, 1926.)

Then, in November 1879, in his diary Sir Hubert refers to the weather being fine at first, followed by snow and frost and yet he still continues to go bathing in the sea. However, he then mentions that Rhoda Garrett's illness is causing considerable anxiety.

Rhoda and Agnes also made new friends in Rustington, including the vicar's family, especially Alice Stansfield, one of the reverend's daughters. They would often spend time together at The Vicarage, The Firs or down at Cudlow House with the Parrys. The cousins spent every summer down in the village thereafter and any other spare time they found available to journey down to the south coast.

The cousins devoted a lot of time visiting Maude, occasionally when Hubert was off on one of his long walks or one of his frequent trips to the vicarage to play tennis. He regularly walked to Arundel, Angmering Park and Highdown Hill and once he even walked the 36-mile round trip to Selsey Bill.

When Rhoda and Agnes moved into 2 Gower Street, they required not only to have a property large enough for their business, but the building had to also accommodate, in the school holidays, Rhoda's half-siblings as well as a housekeeper, a housemaid, a cook and Charles Essam, their live-in painter and decorator. Rhoda's half-siblings Mary Amy (known as Amy), Fydell Edmund (known as Edmund) and the twins Elsie and John stayed during the school holidays as their father was so distressed by the loss of his wife that he was unable to take care of the young family.

Figs. 56 and 57

Front and rear views of 2 Gower Street.

The location of the school vacations changed for Amy, Edmund, John and Elsie when Rhoda and Agnes rented their beautiful cottage in Rustington from 1879. In addition, they also helped to look after Henry and Millicent Fawcett's only child Philippa when Henry and Millicent visited for the latter half of August.

Henry Fawcett's political career over this period was on the rise, so much so that William Gladstone in 1880 appointed him as the Postmaster General and he introduced the parcel post, the sixpenny telegram and postal orders. He also used his leverage as Postmaster General to instigate employment of female medical officers. (Crawford, 1999.)

Memories of this time have survived through a letter written by Edmund to Agnes reminiscing of his time in Rustington, saying, *'I live, with many memories of old Rustington days – the old cottage; you; Rhoda; my boyish tiresomeness and worshippings; the corner in the churchyard; the seat just the other side of the kitchen-garden wall; the picnic breakwater; the moonlit walks; a hundred old pages.'* One delight of the holidays was the sea bathing, under the tutelage at first of Sir Hubert Parry; another was the decoration of a railway carriage, which had been bought as a play room for him and his cousin, Miss Philippa Fawcett. "The Ark," they called it, and it was decorated by them with frescoes of the deluge. [Author's note: This was prior to the story about Milly Molly Mandy and her friends.] It was to be Edmund's lot to live much abroad and in the English colony (South Africa), and he became a devoted lover of the Greater Britain. But no roses were ever so sweet to him as those that bloomed at Rustington, and even the delight of the sea at Muizenburg owed something of its pleasure to memories of the surf in which he had bathed during long summer months at home. (Cook, 1909.)

These happy times would have been in marked contrast to memories of Elton and his parents. His mother, a woman of energy and spirit, had died of consumption when he was a child of seven; his father died six years later, on 21st November 1878 and was buried in Elton Churchyard with his second wife, Mary. (See Fig. 15.)

Edmund did, however, derive his love of poetry from his father and some talent in drawing from his mother and he loved writing letters; whilst he was still at school he would address letters collectively to "Rhodagnes".

One story concerning Edmund (or "F. E. G." as he was also known) was when he returned home from school one Christmas Eve, and found his brother and sisters by no means merry. No Christmas treats were in prospect. He was on this occasion the moneyed man, being the proud possessor of sixpence. *'The children shall all have Christmas presents,'* said he, and they sallied forth to the village shop. It was closed and would not reopen till after bed-time hour at The Rectory. *'I will stand the racket,'* said Edmund, as he sent the others home, staying out himself to expend the sixpence on such little presents for them as it would purchase. His sister preserved hers throughout the rest of her life, as a symbol of the fearlessness and generosity which always distinguished Edmund. This was another trait that was clearly evident in Rhoda. (Cook, 1909.)

In 1878, Rhoda had already been mainly taking care of her half-brothers and sisters for the last six years following their mother's death with the able help of Agnes. The death of her father meant the children were now orphaned, so the care and education of the children was now the responsibility of Rhoda. Following, Rhoda's untimely death in 1882, it was their second cousins Agnes and Millicent who took over this role.

Judging by how the children were to develop (as can be seen in a later chapter), Rhoda, Agnes and Millicent appear to have done an excellent job as stand-in parents!

Most probably the best picture of Rhoda's personality is given by Dame Ethel Smyth (1858-1944). She wrote in her book, *Impressions that Remained*, how they first met, in 1880, as follows:

'Barbara Hamley [later to become Lady Ernle] had often spoke to me of Agnes and Rhoda Garrett, who were among the first women in England to start business on their own account and by that time were well-known house decorators of the Morris school... Late in the autumn Barbara introduced me to these great friends of hers, and during the next two years their house became the focus of my English life owing to the friendship that sprung up between Rhoda and me. [Ethel Smyth was determined to become a composer and spent much of her time studying at the Leipzig Conservatory and later with a private tutor, Heinrich von Herzogenberg, in Leipzig, Germany and she became a close friend of the family.]

Both women were a good deal older than I, how much I never knew – nor wished to know, for Rhoda and I agreed that age and income are relative things concerning which statistics are tiresome and misleading. How shall one describe that magic personality of hers, at once elusive and clear-cut, shy and audacious? – a dark cloud with a burning heart – something that smoulders in repose and bursts into flame at a touch... Though the most alive, amusing, and amused of people, to me at least the sombre background was always there – perhaps because the shell was so obviously too frail for the spirit. One knew of the terrible struggle in the past to support herself and the young brothers and sisters; that she had been dogged by ill health as well as poverty – heroic, unflinching through all. Agnes once said to me: *'Rhoda has had more pain in her life than was good for her,'* but no one guessed that like her brother Edmund – champion of Rhodes, youthful collaborator with Lord Milner, cut off at the zenith of his powers – she carried in her the seeds of tubercular disease. And yet when the end came there was little of surprise in one's grief; thus, again and again had one seen falling stars burn out.

I spoke of her humour; on the whole, I think she was more amusing than anyone else I have ever met – a wit half scornful, always surprising, as unlike everyone else's as was her person... a slim, lithe being, very dark, with deep set burning eyes that I once made her laugh by saying reminded me of a cat in a coal scuttle. Yet cats' eyes are never tender, and hers could be the tenderest in the world. [Author's note: Have a look at the photograph of Rhoda in Fig. 40 to make your own opinion; I for one can see exactly what Dame Ethel meant!]

I always think the feel of a hand as it grasps yours is a determining factor in human relationships, and all her friends must well remember Rhoda's – the soft, soft skin that only dark people have, the firm, wiry, delicate fingers. My reason tells me she was almost plain, but one looked at no one else when she was in a room. There was an enigmatic quality in her witchery behind which the grand lines, the purity and nobility of her soul, stood out like the bone in some enchanted landscape. No one had a more subtle hold on the imagination of her friends, and when she died it was as if laughter, astonishment, warmth, light, mystery, had been cut off at the source. The beauty of the relation between the cousins, and of that home life in Gower Street, remains with us who knew them as certain musical phrases haunt the melomaniac, and but for Agnes, who stood as far as was possible between her and the slings and arrows which are the reward of pioneers, no doubt Rhoda's life would have spent itself earlier. Her every burden, human and otherwise, was shouldered by Agnes, and both had a way of discovering waifs and strays of art more or less worsted by life whose sanctuary their house henceforth became.

Soon after making their acquaintance I went back to Leipzig with a new interest to look forward to for my next stay in England.' (Smyth, 1919.)

In the summer of 1881, Ethel Smyth spent a lot of time with Rhoda and Agnes; she said of the Garretts and Rustington, 'They rented an old thatched cottage at Rustington of which they had made the most perfect of habitations, and the summer holidays and any odd days they could snatch from business were spent there. Rustington was then quite an unfrequented spot – a few straggling cottages and farmhouses, a fine Norman Church, sometimes flicked by spray when south-west gales blew, and an almost deserted beach.

I think I have never been happier in my life than there. An exhausting fight against the stream of prejudice, such as the Garretts had waged for many years, was not to be my portion till later, still we were all three hard-working women, and if circumstances are propitious no one can be more happily lazy than workers. Of course both cousins and all their friends were ardent suffragists, and I wonder now at the patience with which they supported my total indifference on the subject – an indifference I was to make up for thirty years later.

Their great friends the Parrys had a house close by, and besides helping me with invaluable musical criticism and advice Hubert Parry lent me a canoe, in which on very calm days, cautiously dressed in bathing costume, I put to sea. There too I got to know the Fawcetts, and saw how that living monument of courage, the blind Postmaster-General, impresses the country people as he strode up and down the hills, in the company of his wife. I thought Mrs Fawcett rather cold, but an incident that happened the summer after the death of Rhoda, to whom she was devoted, taught me otherwise. One day when I was singing an Irish melody I had often sung at Rustington – *"At the mid hour of night"* – I suddenly noticed that tears were rolling down her cheeks, and presently she got up and quietly left the room. After that for many years I never saw her. Then came the acute Suffrage struggle, during which the gulf that separated Militants from National Unionists belched forth flames, but through all those years, remembering that incident, I always thought of Mrs Fawcett with affection...' (Smyth, 1919.)

One of the next occasions Ethel Smyth met the Garretts was at the Smyths' family home at Frimhurst in the village of Frimley, Surrey in 1882. Ethel wrote of this occasion saying, 'In spite of their arty clothes, the effect of which on Papa's mind I had rather dreaded, they captivated even him; and what is more, Mother's jealousy was instantly swamped in her extraordinary appreciation of Rhoda, whom I think she liked better than all the rest of my friends put together. A great point in their favour with Papa was that they *"braided their hair,"* as he puts it, so as to leave the forehead uncovered, instead of wearing fringes like his daughters and their friends, which he always maintained reduced human beings to the level of apes.' (Smyth, 1919.)

Rhoda on this visit had carved a big R.G. in a beech tree opposite the schoolroom window. Ethel described the schoolroom as such: 'The schoolroom was in the oldest part of the house. The windows, sort of square portholes, to see out of which you had to stand up, were shuttered at night by sliding mirrors. Running under them horizontally on the outside wall were ivy branches as thick as a man's arm, the furry coating of which was worn to the bone by the boots of climbing children.' (Smyth, 1919.)

Fig. 58

A photo given to Ethel Smyth by Rhoda Garrett showing Rhoda with her little half-sister Elsie.

Ethel described Rhoda as also being extremely reserved. Rhoda had asked Ethel, like other correspondents, to destroy all letters sent to her as soon as read. Ethel agreed to do this, so no record of any communication exists now. Fortunately for us, the two letters that Lady Maude Parry received from Rhoda have survived. Ethel always regretted that decision afterwards, as the only things that she possessed following Rhoda's death was a bit of heather, plucked, after Ethel had left England, on Charlotte Bronte's grave, and a little crooked battered stone that Rhoda had once picked up on Rustington beach, remarking that by the time Ethel was 40 her heart would look like that!

Rhoda and Agnes had arranged to visit Ethel in Florence the following Easter in 1883, but alas, this was never to happen. The last time Ethel was to see Rhoda was when Rhoda hurled a forgotten box of a hundred cigarettes to Ethel as her boat left Newhaven Quay in August 1882.

Chapter 13
Rhoda's death

All the way up to and including 1882, Rhoda had been much in demand as a speaker despite her fragile health, and on many occasions stated from the platform the obstacles and overwhelming prejudice she had had to face in an attempt to learn her trade. One of her last major speeches was on 6th May 1880 at St James's Hall, Piccadilly, for the "National Demonstration".

The Graphic said of the meeting that, 'The meeting was an undeniable success, not only in point of numbers – the Hall was crowded, and an overflow meeting was held in a smaller room under the same roof – but in all other respects also. The Presidentess, Viscountess Harberton, was "supported" by a number of lady delegates from important towns in all parts of the country, who filled the platform, whilst the Hall itself was crowded from floor to ceiling with women of all social grades, all earnest and enthusiastic. The meeting had been organised exclusively by women, and the proceedings, in which women alone were permitted to take part, were conducted with the most exemplary regard for the time-honoured usages of ordinary political gatherings. First came the reading of letters of apology from ladies who could not attend; then an address from the Presidentess, setting forth in clear and succinct language the object of the gathering, and then speaker after speaker arose and dilated in eloquent language upon the political disabilities of women; and their determination that sooner or later those disabilities should be removed. The principal resolution declaring that "the franchise attached by law to the occupation or ownership of property liable to imperial and local taxation should be exercised by women in the election of members of Parliament," was carried all but unanimously, the solitary dissentient being a courageous man in the gallery, who by the way must have paid half-a-crown for the opportunity of raising his protesting voice, and whose expression of opinion evoked loud cries of "Turn him out," though whether the suggestion was acted upon we are unable to say. Amongst the speakers, who all addressed both meetings, were Mrs A Arnold, Mrs Patterson, Mrs Webster, Miss R Garrett, Miss Helen Taylor, Miss Becker, Miss Todd,

Miss Downing, and Miss Craigen; and as each one rose, her name was announced to the huge assembly by means of an immense placard, as shown in our engraving.' (See Fig. 59.) (*The Graphic*, 1880.)

Rhoda's fame as a speaker was renowned in the 19th century, as can be seen in the two most common depictions of suffrage meetings both show Rhoda speaking from the platform. (As shown in Figs. 25 and 59.)

Unfortunately, Rhoda's name has not survived as one of the prime instigators for women's suffrage due to later events following Rhoda's death, although her cousin Millicent, who survived to see women get the vote did get her deserved recognition.

However, for the majority of the British public, mention women's suffrage and the only names and events that spring to mind are Emmeline Pankhurst and the woman who threw herself under the King's horse at Epsom on 8th June 1913 (Emily Wilding Davison).

Although, if Rhoda had lived to see the day, I'm sure it would have been Rhoda Garrett who would have been the first name to slip off people's tongues at the mention of women's suffrage!

Fig. 59 Rhoda speaking at "The National Demonstration" on 6th May 1880.

From the end of April 1882, Rhoda and Agnes came down to Rustington as usual. Rhoda's brother, Frank, and his wife Adelaide came over from the Isle of Wight along with their son, Geoffrey, to introduce their daughter Frances, who was only a few weeks old. Frances was christened by the Reverend Stansfield at Rustington Church on 28th May in front of her admiring aunt.

However, on Rhoda's return to Gower Street, her health took a turn for the worse. Telegrams were sent to their friend Alice Stansfield and the Parrys back in Rustington to notify them of the deterioration in Rhoda's health and Agnes sent a similar telegram to Ethel Smyth in Italy.

Dame Ethel Smyth noted that, 'One day in November... a telegram was put into my hand. Rhoda had not written for a week and Agnes had let me know she was rather ill; this message told me she was dead... Italy slipped away from me and for many weeks I only saw Rustington.'

Rhoda lost her brave battle with Typhoid Fever (23 days) and Bronchitis (12 days) on Wednesday 22nd November 1882 at 2 Gower Street at the age of 41. Her death was certified by her cousin Elizabeth Garrett Anderson a day later (although the certificate incorrectly states she was 40 when she died).

Fig. 60

Rhoda Garrett as depicted in *The Cabinet Maker* in 1883 following Rhoda's death.

This period of time is best reflected in the diary of Sir Hubert Parry who made the following entries:

23rd November 1882 (Thursday)

Wild and wet most of the day. Maude came back before lunch... In the evening after dinner I was playing when she walked in with a fixed expression on her face & said something which I did not catch, & handed me a post card from Alice Stansfield, on which were written only the cruel words "No more Hope" Wednesday night. She was my food and brain, but unnaturally quiet, & still both hope that better news may come tomorrow. The last card said poor Rhoda has been very bad however, & the terrible disaster seems almost certain.

24th November 1882

Met the postman in the morning and he handed me a note from Agnes telling me that the blow had fallen, and dear Rhoda had died yesterday. Even in her desolation Agnes thought for Maude, & wanted me with a kindness for her so that I might tell her in the best way to avoid a shock. Maude took it very well, but gradually succumbed under it. Alice Stansfield came later in the day, looking haggard and agonized. Maude and her spent much time together, & I thought best to leave them alone, but they must have been taken with much weepings before their spirits could approach any sort of quietude again. It was a terrible day.

25th November 1882

Most of the morning spent in getting flowers for Rhoda's coffin, poor Alice came again. The funeral was in the afternoon. The sight of those good women Agnes and Mrs Fawcett & Miss Williamson was perfectly agonizing. Agnes was wonderfully calm, but white and angelic looking. Something supernatural. They were all wonderfully restrained; but Mr Stansfield had to make a long stop in reading the kind service & his voice faltered and I had the greatest difficulty in holding myself. I felt on the verge of a veritable explosion. Maude helped me out strangely enough. I think this wonderful collectedness struck me as something so very terrible that it altogether beat me. I looked down into the deep grave and thus a few last flowers and then took Maude home. She went after to see Agnes and I waited for her outside...

26th November 1882

In the morning Maude out to see Alice again, & I took a little walk in my sad humour after leaving her at the vicarage, hard looking at the grave which is prettily covered with wreaths and bunches of flowers. In the afternoon I waited while Maude was at church to take her on to the Firs after, & later Agnes came in the dark and I played her some Bach; the last chorus of the Passion, which she specially wished for, and Chorales & the 2 major Fugues next. She was my calm and quiet. Altogether the saddest sight to see. Her strength and being, & even brightness seem to throw her desolateness, & the breakdown of that beautiful connection between them into stronger relief. It is most piteous. Maude was much lighter on the whole today...

27th November 1882

...Agnes came later and I played a lot of quiet things to her. She keeps marvellously bright...

28th November 1882

Fine but cold. N.W. wind. Directly after breakfast with Maude to say goodbye to Agnes Garrett at the Cottage. It was very sad and it seemed the last farewell to all the happy feelings which centre round that sweet little corner.

The 17-year old Edmund replied to a letter from Lady Maude about his half-sister on Friday 1st December 1882 from Rossall School in Fleetwood, writing the following:

'My Dear Lady Maud

Thank you very much for taking the trouble to write to me, for I like to hear what people think and feel about Rhoda, though I can't say much about it myself. I can hardly understand what has happened – hardly realize that thousands of words, phrases, conversations & sayings, looks and deeds, and all the things that I remember so well, are now nothing more than a memory. It seems to me very hard. What you say is exactly true. She was different from everyone else. Others might be good, others earnest, but there never was another Rhoda, there is only one, and I think there never will be another. That shows her genius; but the myriad of things that show her perseverance & hard work & unselfishness are to me the most comforting and valuable. We are born with talents; and if we have genius, it is ours from birth; I can see little to love in it, however much we admire; it is steadfast earnest use of abilities that strikes me most; it seems so unattainable, so much above. Rhoda was one among a thousand in her wonderful charm and influence & genius but she was one among a million in the use she made of these; – I hardly know yet what a hole her loss has made in my life. She had such a Purpose about my life, that I believe she would have given half her own to see me with the power – which I never possessed – of acting so as to fulfil it. You say truly, indeed, that she made as all perfect, in the sense that without her we feel as if we had lost the better half of ourselves. As for Belief, – I only know that what St James says of it, – that "the devils also believe and shudder!" has a deeper meaning to my mind than was ever meant, I think – judge her by her fruits, – and to every "good" "respectable" "pious" churchgoer that "pities" her, I give the lie, and I say they may thank their God if they are worthy to touch the hem of her garment! I do not know about meeting again, I do not think I am up to that level; but I do think, that if the very memory alone of all the happiness she has wrought for others is not making her happy herself, there is no justice in heaven and earth! Thank you for your real & valuable sympathy: I think she lives in Agnes, and I her deeds. "The actions of the just smell sweet and blossom in their dust."

Yours gratefully

Edmund Garrett'

Meanwhile, back in Italy, the distraught Ethel Smyth was reminiscing about Rhoda and Rustington saying, 'There are few spots on earth, I imagine, of which anyone can say: "There, at least, I was perfectly happy," but whenever the beach at Rustington suddenly stands before my mind's eye, that thought swims up with the vision... I am glad to think of her lying within the shadow of the old church, close to the stretch of sea we both loved better than any other...'

She then went on to add, 'Almost nightly I dreamed of my dead friend, dreams such as this: "Listen; I shall go away tomorrow, and if I tell you I shall be coming back again in a month, you know you cannot die till I do!" and she answered with the old amused gleam in her eye: "Of course I can't; that's rather a good idea – go by all means." And then I would awake, as tens of thousands awake nightly while the earth is turning smoothly round the sun, asking myself: "How can I bear this?" The only key that opens a way out of the torture-house, acceptance, seemed lost for ever. "Will talking of Rhoda," I asked Lisl, "ever be like talking of last year's toothache?" That question I can answer now; speaking for myself, certain tragedies in one's life can be put away, not thought of hardly for years if you choose it shall be so; but the moment you let your mind dwell on them the old ache comes back, and is mastered by weapons

Time has put into your hands. One gets over everything... and nothing.'

In 1883, Ethel Smyth travelled back to England and wrote, 'How the sadness of that return to England came back to me the other day, when passing through Frimhurst, which is to let, I sought and found traces of the big "R.G." Rhoda had carved in the beech tree opposite the schoolroom window! Of course my first visit was to Rustington, my first walk to the churchyard. Nothing wrings the heart more sharply than remembering the jokes of a recently lost friend; as I laid on the grave a wreath I had made of the heather and many tinted ferns she had admired round Frimhurst just a year ago, it flashed across me that she had once said I handled flowers as if I were buckling up the straps of a harness!... In the hall her coat was still hanging, her stick still standing in its old place, and her favourite dog had learned, as dogs will, not to miss her... On her writing-table was a caricature I had drawn of myself going away in a rage from the Parrys, because he wouldn't play me Beethoven's Opus III when I wanted him to, and under it written in her strange, strong handwriting: "Ethel, the versatile wax statue, going away from Knight's Croft." ...And the beach without her... and the hopeless bewilderment of a first great sorrow relived on the spot where you had been so happy! ...of Agnes, who carried on Rhoda's work and responsibilities, and is alive now to see their fruition, I will only say that grief such as hers makes me half ashamed to have spoken so much of my own.'

One can only imagine the hole it left in Agnes following Rhoda's death; Agnes was always there to support the star speaker for women's suffrage during the 1870s and 1880s and had been there for her in her times of grief and illness as well as the happier times and through their work together.

One object, which now appears to have been lost or destroyed, that used to be in "The Firs" in Rustington was a embroidery made by Agnes in her grief as her own memorial to Rhoda, as seen in Fig. 64 below. She intimates her feelings for Rhoda and describes her qualities in a few well-chosen words. There are two points to note on the embroidery, firstly that the year of birth was incorrect, so I believe that Agnes, Millicent and Elizabeth (remembering that the age on the death certificate was wrong) didn't know she was actually born in 1841 not 1842, and secondly, the K inside the circle is puzzling; I can only presume that this was originally an R for Rhoda and a stitch had come undone or it had been poorly transcribed. Perhaps the readers themselves can find a more logical solution to this.

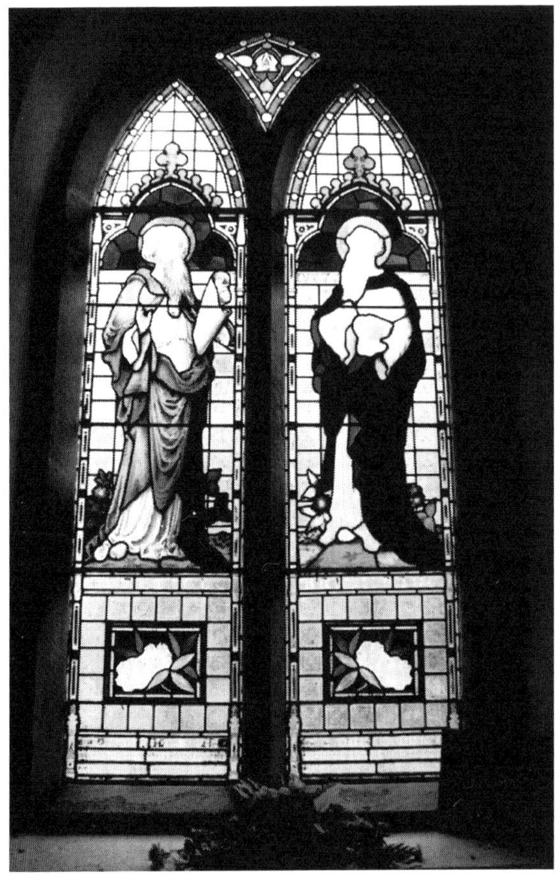

Fig. 61 (left)

The memorial window on the north wall in Elton Church for Rhoda Garrett, her father John and her mother Elizabeth.

The window has the prophet Ezekiel, representing the Old Testament on the left and St Paul, representing the New Testament on the right.

Figs. 62 and 63 (below)

The inscription reads from left to right on the top/ middle and bottom of Figs. 62 and 63:

In memory of the Revnd J. F. Garrett B.A. XI years rector of this parish died A.D. MDCCCLXXVIII and of Elizabeth his wife died A.D. MDCCCLIII and of Rhoda their daughter died A.D. MDCCCLXXXII.

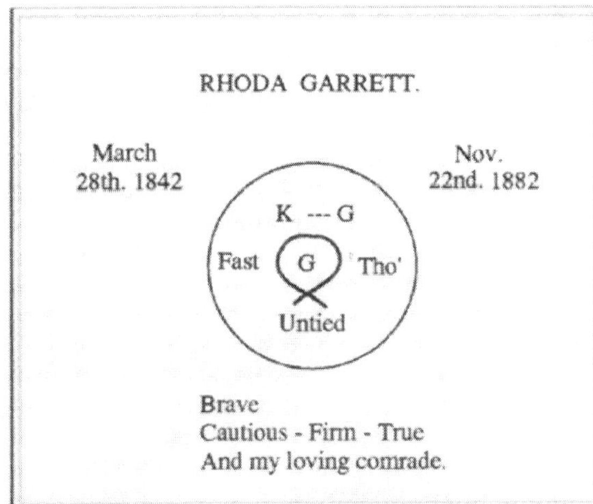

RHODA GARRETT.
March
28th. 1842
Nov.
22nd. 1882
K --- G
Fast
G
Tho'
Untied
Brave
Cautious - Firm - True
And my loving comrade.

Fig. 64

Copy of the design that was on the embroidery found at "The Firs" made by Agnes Garrett following Rhoda's death.

The only written evidence of Agnes's grief and her plans following Rhoda's death were in a letter to Lady Maude on Monday 11th December 1882. She wrote: 'I know all she was to me helping me perpetually from sinking into commonplace aims & low ideals. I feel as if I were an ear of wheat that has been threshed & robbed of all the living grains. It is this that has made me shrink so from going on with our work – as if I should have no freshness no originality no delicacy to offer people – in fact that I should be that which she hated so – a charlatan. But no one else seems to think so – they didn't know what she was so entirely as I do – & for the sake of the two boys I have determined to go on at any rate for the present. I only really made up my mind about this on Saturday...' And go on she did!

Although there is a memorial for Rhoda and her family in her birth town, there is no such memorial to this day in Rustington and in fact there is no sign of her grave to be seen in the churchyard. Many of the older graves have been moved or simply destroyed. Considering the importance and high regard that the village held for Rhoda, especially as a personal friend of the Reverend Stansfield, the vicar of Rustington, it seems more than surprising that no sign of the grave can be seen today. I believe from the information available that the grave was in the south-west corner of the graveyard, situated fairly close to the lych-gate between the footpath and the flint wall, which would have bordered The Grange.

Perhaps the grave was removed subsequently because of her heavy involvement in the suffrage movement. There is no way that the Reverend Stansfield, who died in 1907, would have had it removed, but could it have been the next vicar, the Reverend Crosland (vicar between 1908 and 1940)? He was a much more controversial figure, and a fully paid-up member of the fascist movement prior to the start of the Second World War and he was a friend of William Joyce (aka Lord Haw Haw). William Joyce regularly stayed at the vicarage with the vicar's son who was interned under Defence Regulation 18B during the war. However, it could very easily be anyone else with a personal grudge against the movement. The grave certainly wasn't there after the war when a plan was made of all the gravestones. However, it is my intention to put this to rights in the not too distant future by having a memorial placed somewhere in the village on behalf of both Rhoda Garrett and her cousin Agnes.

I mentioned in the introduction that two pieces of music had been written and dedicated to Rhoda.

The first of these was by Hubert Parry. His fine setting of James Shirley's poem, *Death the Leveller*, a magnificent funeral ode, *The Glories of our Blood and State*, was written in 1883 to the memory of Rhoda Garrett and performed at the Gloucester Festival in the summer of that year. However, when Henry Fawcett died the year after, the work subsequently published in 1885 was dedicated "To the memory of Rhoda Garrett and Henry Fawcett".

Fig. 65 Hubert Parry's tribute to Rhoda Garrett.

The *String Quintet in E Major* was the second piece; it was written by Ethel Smyth in 1883 and was the very first of Smyth's works to be published. The first edition was printed in Leipzig by CF Peters in 1884 and bore the following dedication on its front cover: "To the memory of Rhoda Garrett."

It is a testament to the remarkable character of Rhoda Garrett that two such distinguished composers chose to dedicate their works to her!

Fig. 66 Ethel Smyth's tribute to Rhoda Garrett.

Chapter 14
Rhoda's half-brothers and sisters

I have already detailed the lives of the two brothers and sister from her father's first marriage and the first born from the second marriage, John Fergusson Garrett, who died at the age of six.

I will now turn to Rhoda's remaining half-brothers and half-sisters who survived her.

Rhoda was 21 when Mary Amy Garrett (Amy) was born in Elton. She received little formal education but some musical education, first at home and then in London where she moved at the age of sixteen. She was to go on and study music in Germany; one wonders if Rhoda's wide circle of friends had some input here.

Amy's brother Edmund, three years her junior, boarded at the Spondon Preparatory School in Derbyshire following his mother's death. At the age of 14 he won a scholarship to Rossall School in Lancashire. It was at this public school that he found out about Rhoda's death and from here he wrote the letter to Lady Maude, as seen in the last chapter. Edmund's people following his parents' deaths had been his half-sister, Rhoda, and his cousins Agnes Garrett and Mrs Fawcett. Rhoda dearly loved Edmund and that love was reciprocated. 'The poor boys!' were among the last words Rhoda uttered, for she had made Edmund and his younger brother John her special care. On Rhoda's death, primarily for her sake, but with an equal love on her own part, Agnes assumed this charge.

Edmund was indebted, not only for the generosity of Agnes and Mrs Fawcett (who came to live with Agnes after the death of her husband Professor Fawcett) to pay his school and college fees launching him into a promising career, but also for the influence of a cultured home. He always said he owed Millicent much of the intellectual stimulus and many of the ideas which he held most earnestly. So, it is not surprising that he became an ardent advocate of the woman's suffrage movement.

However, it was Agnes who acted as mother, sister and friend to Edmund through his life as Millicent had her daughter Philippa to look after and it is said that he repaid her care by unfailing confidence, comradeship and affection. He dedicated his version of Ibsen's *Brand* to

Agnes, which read as follows: (Cook, 1909.)

'To AGNES. For thousands of readers the Agnes of Ibsen's Brand, like the Agnes of Dickens in "David Copperfield," must have idealised a name which surely no author could well bestow save on a pure and beautiful creation. For me, not even namesakes such as these can add to your name one new ray of consecration or of loveliness.'

It was at Trinity College, Cambridge, that he first met John Badley. John Badley reminisced of their time at Trinity saying, 'Edmund Garrett and I must have been up at Trinity together for a year or so before we met. My first recollection of him is, I think seeing him at the chapel services, and wondering who he was. There was something in his face, open, boyish, full of life, yet with the unmistakable stamp of thought and decision and purpose, that attracted me to him at once. Inquiry showed that he was of my own year, a keen speaker at debates, and the life and soul of a freshmen's literary society...' (Cook, 1909.)

Edmund and John Badley became best friends. When Degree Day came, Edmund's sister Amy came up to Cambridge and this later became a bond to draw Edmund and John's friendship still closer.

In the summer of 1887, Edmund turned up at the offices of the *Pall Mall Gazette*, which was then in Northumberland Street and asked for work. In Edmund Garrett's book by ET Cook he showed what was so evident in Rhoda and the other Garretts' spirit and ingenuity. This is what followed in the *Pall Mall Gazette* office. 'Mr Stead, most accessible of editors, received him kindly, but had no opening on his staff and was very busy. For once he was in no mood to talk, even to so pleasant-spoken a young man; but his visitor had come for an interview and meant to have it. Since the great man showed no disposition to play the interviewer, his caller assumed the part himself, and settling himself comfortably down in the chair drew the editor on into general conversation. He left the office with no promise of work or encouragement other than such as an interview with so genial an editor might inspire. "I saw he didn't think much of me," said Garrett afterwards; "why should he? A pasty-faced undergraduate who thought he wrote verses!" He returned to Cambridge, and spent the evening in composing, in the style so far as might be of Mr Stead himself, an "Interview with the Editor of the *Pall Mall Gazette*," adorned with a pen-and-ink sketch of him too, with his feet up on the mantelpiece of his sanctum. It was posted to the editor, who perceived at once that here was a young man of spirit and audacity.

wielding moreover – in spite of a University education the pen of a ready and picturesque writer. Garrett was sent for, and was given a commission for a descriptive article. This was the beginning of a connection with the *Pall Mall Gazette* and with its off-shoot, *The Westminster* which, with interruptions from ill-health, lasted for eight years.' (Cook, 1909.)

He, like Rhoda, had a delicate constitution. In 1887, he had been admitted to the West London Hospital suffering from a sharp attack of pleurisy. The ill-health referred to in the above paragraph was that he was diagnosed with TB in the autumn of 1889. So Mr Stead sent him to the warmer climate of South Africa for a year to report on the problems there, its people and industries.

F.E.G.'s holidays whilst he was working for the *Pall Mall Gazette* were spent with his sisters and with college friends abroad in Norway. His best friend wrote, 'No one could more keenly enjoy the delights of an open-air holiday than he always did; and in Norway we had them to the full – scrambling to our heart's content; days' tramps in scenes of endless variety and endless beauty; bathing now in crystal-clear river-pools, now in a fjord chill with glacier river or warmed with the gulf-stream, or, "to see what it felt like", in the stinging and blinding drive of the spray of a giant waterfall; belated on unknown mountains, caught in storms on mountain-lakes; finding everywhere the warmest hospitality and, in those less travelled parts to which we mainly kept, a people absolutely unspoilt and unsophisticated. The charm of country and people awoke interest in its literature, and led, later on, to his translation of *Brand* and of others of Ibsen's poems; and he always looked back to the times we had together in Norway, not only as the best of holidays, but also as a happy influence in his life. A second visit to Norway in the following year, completed the spell that "der gammle land" had thrown over us.' (Cook, 1909.)

So it is easy to see why Edmund dedicated his version of Ibsen's *Brand* to Agnes.

Edmund's sense of humour with his friends is characterised in a letter he wrote to his friend John Badley, which he wrote in a mock serious way as follows: (Cook, 1909.)

'Dear J.H.B., – I very much want to answer properly your two splendid letters, for which thanks a thousand times and for all that underlies them. I should have answered before but for work – a week away at

Manchester – neuralgia, &c. I will write soon. But meanwhile something rather serious has come up, which I must write about at once.

Dear old John and I have been having some talks about your name.

We think "Jack" sounds somehow too light and flippant. If you come to think of it, there isn't really much to choose between it and "Jamie". "Jack the Ripper", for instance, is a rather too ripping association. But first I should tell you that we have written to Henry about calling him by that name. "Harry" is so awfully un-serious, you know. A man called Harry is blasted from the font. I think it is easy to understand the influence of these little things on character. Now "Henry" calls up grand historical associations. The mere name is a trumpet. We both hope it will be of great help to him in his life.

Have you heard from my sister Mary lately – by the way, I haven't told you yet, have I, about our agreeing to call her by this name? It is her first name, you know; and we think "Amy" doesn't describe her at all. One wants a name to be more than a mere way of calling one. It should convey a testimonial, a picture, a criticism of life. "Amy" suggests only the "shallow-hearted" associations of Locksley Hall.

Now about yourself. You see we want "John" for Withers, and Henry is already occupied for the friend whom, in our thoughtless days, when we were content to take names as we found them, we used to call "Harry". So that unless your second name turns out to be Habakkuk or Hezekiah or Halicarnassus – something for the mind to feed on – we shall be rather up a genealogical tree in the matter of nomenclature. We think, both of us, that it would really be the best thing for us all to meet and talk it over – say up at Newcastle, which seems the most natural and simple thing now that we are all pretty well massed in the South of England.

Please write about this, and send it on to Mary and Henry. Love from John.

Believe me, Hezekiah, old man,

Yours, FYDELL'

In 1890, his elder sister Amy had gone to visit old friends in Nordrach with John Badley (who Edmund called Jack!). Jack and Amy were to later marry. It was here his sister saw the sanatorium where the open-air cure for phthisis (TB, or consumption as it was also called) had been practiced for some years.

In the June of 1892, Edmund went with Amy and John to Nordrach (in the Black Forest region of south-west Germany) in search of a cure to the disease which had caused the death of his mother. He stayed in Nordrach until the spring of 1893.

It was in a small town near Nordrach that Jack and Amy were married in November 1892 so that Edmund could be present.

Edmund wrote the following letter to Agnes detailing the wedding in the Black Forest:

'To MISS AGNES GARRETT November 8

"It has them," as the Burgomaster choicely expressed it yesterday. It took us two days, but it is done, and here followeth the true and particular account. Yesterday was the State's only; today, the Church's. In Germany it's only the State that matters; no church can register; so by rights it was yesterday, the 7th, that they were married, but we all agreed to count it from to-day, since the Church still keeps the poetry to herself and the State was very prosaic indeed. Yesterday morning the Herr Doctor drove Jack and Amy and me down to Nordrach. As we passed the old Burgomaster's house two white shirt-sleeves appeared strikingly at the window: his Frau was helping him on with his black coat. This abashed us a little, for Jack and I were very much in mufti – indeed I wore knickerbockers with plum-coloured stockings. At the Rathhaus further down the street we got out and waited. At last the Burgomaster appeared – we thought the black coat must have split down the back and needed sewing up again. Into the Rathhaus we went – a large building including schoolroom, from which latter could be heard the sing-song of the children at their lessons. The Burgomaster was very cordial and genial, and we all sat about the table. The sheaf of certificates which we had accumulated to show our bona-fides were produced on a file, and Jack and Amy were instructed to say Ja to whatever was asked of them. Then the Burgomaster got down their names on a private note of his own in phonetic spelling (Schon hedn badli, &c. &c.); and explaining parenthetically that it was the first time he had ever married an English couple, prepared to ask the fateful question. First, however, he dismissed all smiles from his clean-shaven old face, and with a child-like expression slipped over his grey head what looked like a silver watch-chain with a florin at the end. Thus invested with full municipal dignity, he addressed "Schon" and "Emi" and asked them if each really wished to marry the other? Each replied "Ja," and – behold it was done! The old man doffed his chain, resumed the merely human rôle, and shaking them paternally by the hand, pronounced some appropriate wish which Jack breezily "danke'd," as who should say "It's all in the day's work". Then to the Inn, where the representative of civic dignity joined us, and we all partook of some of the nastiest wine which family devotion ever brought its reluctant lips to smack over.

And then we went home to dinner. The Kranks were all eyes, especially when the Herr Doctor addressed Amy down the table as "Mrs Badley". "Never mind," quoth Jack, "when we are well through this we shall be armed with triple brass!" In Amy's place was a pretty little stand made of fir-sprigs bearing a gratulatory card of colour and design which even German art could hardly beat. This was a friendly Krank's offering. But there was more to come. That evening we were all bidden to the Speiseaal at 6.45, and sat as in a theatre – no tables, and a cold collation (of ample size) served in our seats. Jack and Amy were put in the centre chairs of the front rank, but we had managed to protest against "thrones". First, the children did a little play, which was encored – and very prettily they did it. It represented a young man going round a family to ask for the hand of the daughter and being referred from one to another in a House-that-Jack-built sort of way. Then a boy called Karl got up as a geigerl (I won't swear to spelling), or Viennese Anglo-maniac masher, recited a little ballad composed by one of the Kranks with a comic English burden of "Oh jes!" [As it was spelt in the MS.] This was very topical; it described Jack coming from England in cavalier style, and reminded "Mees Eme" not to forget at the appropriate moment to answer "Oh jes!" They (the pair) sat through this beautifully; I felt the "martyr's stalls" weren't good enough for them. But the fact is everyone was brimming over with good humour and good wishers, and nobody had a doubt but that the whole thing was the very heart's desire of the bride and bridegroom in whose honour it was done. The evening ended with fireworks outside and the salute-gun which we had on the Grand Duke's birthday.

This morning we arose early and showed the breakfasting Kranks what we could do when we tried in the smart line. Amy in all her glory, Jack in new clo' and I in my best dove coloured bags and new shoes and the Fur Coat over all! The drive to Gengenbach is over the hills, lovelier even than the one to Biberach-Zell. They both looked very quiet and happy. I felt I must try to represent all of us, and could not succeed in representing what I felt myself. There was no sun, but it was not dull;

fresh and cool air, and the last of the autumn glories looking almost like sunlight from wood to wood till we got to Gengenbach. This is a perfect gem of the Black Forest: picturesque streets, towers, gates and so on. But the "Evangelical Church" turned out to be a little newish place, not unlike the chapels in Littlehampton Cemetery. Alas for Protestant architecture! However, inside it proved to be plain, simple, almost pretty. The Pfarrer's house was close by. He was a gentlemanly little man, a Lutheran German edition of my father. We felt that he would do very well. After looking over the certificate from the Burgomaster, he led the way to the church. The Pfarrer appeared in a neat black gown with white bands, and read a homily from a book in resonant sonorous German. Then he motioned those two to the altar steps, where each had to respond "Ja" to the familiar question. They took each other's hands, first kneeling on the steps and then standing up – there is no ring in the German ceremony. In a quarter of an hour the service was ended. Afterwards Jack told me the service seemed to him as beautiful as the English without its defects. I had only understood parts myself.

I'm sorry to say that while the Pfarrer was pronouncing sentences and putting "Amens" at the end of each, I was somehow reminded of Karl last night and his "Oh jes" after each verse. But when they joined hands I had to try to think of Karl to prevent my eyes filling with tears. They two were just quietly happy, facing the new life full of hope and faith, and I did not want to show more emotion than they did.' (Cook, 1909.)

Fig. 67

Edmund Garrett in 1895.

Edmund was to sufficiently recover to return to South Africa in 1895; his articles on South African affairs and personalities were published in a book and this brought him fame as a journalist. He was then offered the post as editor of *The Cape Times*. This was only a few months prior to the Jameson Raid, so he found himself embroiled in the turmoil of these times. He met, consulted and interviewed various personalities of the time in South Africa such as Cecil Rhodes, Rudyard Kipling, President Paul Kruger, Sir Percy Fitzpatrick and Sir Arthur Milner.

F.E.G. also became a member of the Cape Parliament; however, although his health had improved initially, he still suffered from tuberculosis. In 1899, Edmund had to resign this post following a serious lung haemorrhage. He returned to England in the autumn of 1900, where he was put under the medical charge of Dr Jane Walker, firstly at a farmhouse (Maltings), and afterwards in her sanatorium at Nayland, East Anglia, until early 1903. It was here that he met Ellen Marriage. They were to be married on 26th March 1903. Ellen took him away from the sanatorium and they set up home in St Ives in Cornwall before moving to Wiverton Acre near Plympton in Devon from June 1904. Ellen nursed Edmund at home until his death from tuberculosis on 10th May 1907 at the age of 41. (The same age Rhoda died.)

Fig. 68 Memorial to F.E.G. in Elton Church.

Following their return to England, Amy's husband John was considering the possibilities of reforming public-school education. He was of the opinion that the education they provided was too narrow and did little to care for the pupils as individuals as well as the encouragement of bullying. So in 1893, John and Amy along with Osbert Powell and Winifred Cobb, who was a good friend of Amy's, took the brave step of opening a new school in a house they rented on Bedales Hill at Lindfield in Sussex. This is where the name "Bedales" originated. Osbert and Winifred were soon to marry.

One of the first three pupils at the school was Rhoda's younger brother, Frank's son Geoffrey. Edmund, despite his ongoing illness at the time of its opening, became very involved in the school. He designed the first school badge and the library bookplate. This design included "a rose for England, and a bee for hardwork". John Badley and F.E.G. wrote the first pamphlet together, setting out the aims and ideals of the school. Bedales was to be an unconventional school, being run along progressive lines in a democratic way, so instead of concentrating on the classics they put more emphasis on science, modern languages, art, music and drama.

Amy was in charge of music as she had taught it at Gateshead High School following her music studies in Germany and she would often play her favourite composer, Bach; she was described as a fine musician. One of her former pupils wrote of her saying, 'She played Bach with veneration, with strict and selfless devotion. Life burned with an intense flame in that small and fragile body.' (Crawford, 2002.)

The first production at Christmas 1893 was very ambitious, that of *Macbeth*. Banquo was played by Edmund and Lady Macbeth was played by Amy's younger sister, Elsie. Elsie painted some of the scenery and made some of the costumes. Thanks to both Rhoda and Agnes, Elsie had studied art at the Royal Female School of Art and the Slade School of Art in London before finishing her studies in Florence, Italy. Elsie then became an art teacher and artist. Like both Rhoda and Amy, Elsie was slight of build, but with a forceful personality. (Crawford, 2002.)

On 3rd October 1894, John and Amy had a baby boy called John Edmund. (He was later known as Jock and he died in 1974. Jock married Marie Ferrars MacTaggart in 1922; however, they didn't have any children.)

During the early years of Bedales, the summer camps for the school were held at "The Firs" in Rustington, where Rhoda and Agnes leased and that Agnes was still at following Rhoda's death.

The first mathematics and science master at Bedales was Charles Emmanuel Rice; he had been at Bedales from the start up until 1897. He left to become the first headmaster of King Alfred's School, Hampstead. He ran the school in the same way as Bedales. He did return to Bedales in 1908. (Crawford, 2002.)

On 17th April 1898, Charles Rice married Rhoda's youngest half-sister Elsie at Rustington Church. The service was taken by the Reverend Stansfield.

After being persuaded by Edmund and his wife Amy, John decided to use a co-educational system for the school and this was the first genuinely co-educational school in country.

When the first few girls arrived at Bedales, Amy urged them 'to work ceaselessly for women's rights, not to marry the first man who asked them and not to wear corsets'. (Crawford, 2002.)

Amy was obviously a keen supporter of her cousin Millicent Fawcett's suffragists but also supported the militant suffragettes under Emmeline Pankhurst. She was unable to be a militant herself as she had to consider the reputation of Bedales above the cause and the fact that she was too frail to take part. However, she did give financial support to the suffragettes when Emmeline Pankhurst was in hiding from the police.

Rhoda would have been so proud of them all!

Fig. 69

John and Amy Badley.

Bedales School then moved from Lindfield, near Haywards Heath in Sussex, to Steep, near Petersfield in Hampshire, when John Badley and Osbert Powell bought a country estate there in 1899. The school opened there in 1900.

Elsie joined her husband at the school in 1908 as housemistress of a newly expanded girls' house, Steephurst; she also taught both botany and art. This position she held for three years.

Charles and Elsie later moved to Coventry when Charles qualified as a doctor; by this time they had two children, Gabriel and Rosemary. Gabriel was a pilot in "The Great War" and died in a plane crash at the age of nineteen. Rosemary married Dr Charles Hawthorn and they had four children, Sheila, Nigel and the twins Janette and John. The family emigrated to Cape Town, South Africa, in 1932.

Elsie's grandson, Nigel Hawthorne became a well-known actor playing the part of Humphrey Appleby, the Permanent Secretary in *Yes Minister*.

Elsie followed the family out to South Africa a year later after becoming separated from her husband where she lived for the rest of her life, firstly in Rondebosch then at Camps Bay with her daughter Rosemary and her husband Charles. Elsie was living on monies earned from her painting and an annuity of £200 left to her by Agnes.

Fig. 70

Watercolour painted by Elsie Garrett Rice.

Elsie was an excellent artist, especially with watercolours of wild flowers. She was to have exhibitions which led to her being commissioned to illustrate a book by RH Compton, called *Wild Flowers of the Cape of Good Hope*, published in 1951. Elsie died at the age of 90 on 2nd July 1959.

Amy Badley died at the age of 94 on 30th October 1956 and was cremated at Woking, Surrey.

Amy's husband John allowed the school to evolve and was known as the "Chief" by both staff and the pupils. He retired at the age of 70 to Cholesbury, near Tring, having been headmaster for 42 years. He died on 6th March 1967 at the age of 102.

Very little is known of Elsie's twin brother John, apart from that he emigrated to Hawthorn, Victoria, Australia, living with his wife Jane (known as Jenny) at 34 Fletcher Street, Hawthorn, and working as a wood merchant and then a rancher. He did return to England staying at 2 Gower Street when he enlisted into the army for "The Great War" on 29th December 1915. However, the exposure to the weather caused a dilation to the heart so he was discharged on medical grounds a few months later on 13th April 1916. He returned to Australia and died at the age of 54 on 20th September 1923 in Hawthorn.

Chapter 15
Rhoda's Legacy

So what legacy did Rhoda leave for her family, friends, the places associated with her and the women's suffrage movement?

Without going into great details about the events in the late nineteenth and early twentieth century, I will concentrate on the specific people and places relating to Rhoda Garrett and what direct influence both consciously and sub-consciously she affected.

As we have seen, Rhoda had been helped by her Suffolk cousins when endeavouring to find employment in the early years, especially from Louie, Elizabeth and Elizabeth's friend Emily Davies and was welcomed into their Aldeburgh homes. She also spent time at Newson Garrett's malting business in Snape and both Rhoda and her cousin's ancestors' business in Leiston, Suffolk. So, she had no hesitation in giving back to the area what she could on her various visits, including helping with stalls at various fundraising events. It was also in Suffolk, namely in Ipswich and Framlingham, that she gave her first two talks on behalf of women's suffrage.

Rustington continued to be a place that the Garrett family would spend quite a lot of time. Agnes carried on renting "The Firs" after Rhoda's death up until 1899; Rhoda's younger half-sister Elsie married at Rustington Church and the summer camps for Bedales were held at "The Firs". Agnes then rented from the Wellesley family "Pound Cottage", just over the road from "The Firs" for another five years. Agnes finally broke her ties with the village in 1905, on her retirement from the business, which she had run successfully following Rhoda's death, and gave all her (& Rhoda's) furniture from Pound Cottage to Rhoda's half-brother Edmund.

JM Barrie rented "The Firs" not long after Agnes had moved out; it is said that his book *Sentimental Journey* was written at the cottage.

Elizabeth Garrett Anderson also rented a summerhouse in Rustington between 1906 and 1912, this was Little Ffynches. This kept alive the association between the village and the Garrett family.

Many suffrage meetings were held in Rustington, often at Ffynches Lodge, with the Wellesleys, sometimes at Cudlow House. These meetings took place both before and after Rhoda's death.

Sir Hubert and Lady Maude Parry were living at Knightscroft House, Rustington with their two daughters, Dorothea (Dolly) and Gwendoline (Gwen). The first time that Sir Hubert was to attend a women's suffrage meeting was in December 1874; it was believed that his interest in the movement had been enlisted by his friendship with Rhoda and Agnes. Rhoda was one of the speakers at this first meeting Sir Hubert attended and he said Rhoda spoke very well. Sir Hubert's sympathies to the cause were genuine despite his distaste for the militant tactics adopted in the second decade of the 20th century. Lady Maude Parry, who had a very strong character, and as can be seen in the introduction, an eloquent writer, would often lead marches and chair meetings in support of women's suffrage.

One such meeting was due to be held at Knightscroft House on 12th August 1914 just after the start of "The Great War". However, the nature of the meeting was changed as can be seen in the following article under the heading, "Suffragists and the War – How they will help – Sir Harry Johnston and the German Emperor" and gives an interesting insight as to what the thoughts of the nation were at the beginning of the war as follows:

'More ladies than there could be found chairs for gathered in the pleasant grounds of Lady Maude Parry's Rustington home on Wednesday afternoon to hear an address by Sir Harry H Johnston, K.C.M.G., relative to Women's Work in Time of War.

The meeting which proved of a most pleasant nature, was held under the auspices of the local branch of the National Union of Women's Suffrage Societies. Lady Parry presided and the others who took a prominent part in it were Miss Urlin, Mr. T. Dove Keighley, Mr Israel Zangwill and the Hon. Mrs Bertrand Russell.

Lady Parry, in opening, said it was to have been a suffrage meeting but they had had orders from Mrs Fawcett that there should be no more political meetings until the end of the war. So, they were going to work for the good of the country, through their organisation, in an endeavour to alleviate the terrible distress that might come upon England. Lady Parry went on to show that in some quarters unemployment had already trebled. Much of the export trade was closing down and the number of other trades still comparatively uninjured grew scarcer. She had been told by a suffrage friend that thousands of poor London women were out of work, but she was proud to say she had also been told that their societies were going to their rescues in a splendid fashion (applause). By their activity at the present juncture they would prove England that suffrage women were at least as patriotic as any other woman. (Hear hear.)

Some Good Advice.

She urged those before her to employ poor women for as many things as they could. Let them not do needlework themselves; they would do far better if they paid people to do it for them. There were many things they could do if they wished. They could drive carts and so help poor tradespeople, they could help in the harvesting, and in fact, do all kinds of things; but don't let them sew.

Then they should think of how to relieve the destitution that might spring up around them and, of charities which were suffering just at present. Lady Parry referred to the heroic part some Belgian women were playing in the war; to such glorious achievements of such heroines as Joan of Arc; and spoke confidently of what women would do in the times that lay before them.

If women in all countries had the vote she thought one result would be that war and the building of armament as they knew them at the present time would be done away with. Was it not a terrible thing that in this twentieth century, nations, with all their boasted civilization should settle their disputes in this horrible cruel and disgusting manner? (Applause.) [We are now in the 21st century and even now, with women in so many countries having equal opportunities, very little has changed on this front!] But they knew that so far as Sir Edward Grey was concerned he had no alternative but to fight seeing that our honour was involved with the blow struck at little Belgium and we could not abandon our friendship with France.

Sir Harry Johnston's Speech.

Sir Harry Johnston opened an interesting speech by remarking that when he promised to speak that afternoon they were to talk about something else, namely, the question of votes for women, but when the terrible news fell so suddenly upon them, Lady Maude Parry at once decided to call a meeting for the discussion of the duty of women in war time. That would be the scope of their thoughts and of the afternoon speeches. The war would bring on most of the countries of Europe, whether victorious or vanquished, almost unparalleled suffering, yet he believed that it would bring in its train good things that would go far to compensate for the bad and would perhaps do away altogether warfare between nations, of the present kind killing of one another by murderous weapons, or by starvation. This was a crisis in the history of Great Britain for a comparison they would have to go back 100 years. But in those days, it was far less easy than to-day to reach our inviolate isle. Between while steam had created a revolution. They could not tell how the drift of the present war should go. They could not say whether the victories would come quickly or whether it would be dragged out for months. However, he felt confident of this much that however fortune might at first favour the Germans armies, Germany would never succeed in conquering Great Britain and France. (Cheers.)

Too Good to be True.

The war would bring many surprises. It had brought them already. Who of their writers, in anticipation of this struggle, had ever written to predict that Belgium would unaided be able to hold up the entire striking force of the German Empire for 10 days? The fewer predictions they made the better. In this particular they could set an example to the rest of England, not to talk thoughtlessly, but to be most cautious lest they should become scaremongers, and to be careful not to circulate extravagantly good news or extravagantly bad news.

Sir Harry here obliged with one or two of his own experiences. He was told only the night before that the German Emperor had been shot by one of his own soldiers. The person who gave him the information when asked what foundation he had for it attributed it to a source that seemed thoroughly trustworthy. Judge of his deep disappointment when on receiving the papers that morning he found the story to be incorrect. He had been hoping from the bottom of his heart the news was true. They should be most careful not too quickly to believe what they saw in the papers and they should not forget that things might get worse. A German ship might even attempt landing in West Sussex. Under all circumstances they would best serve the country by keeping cool, calm and collected. In that respect they had lessons to learn from their children, the Boy Scouts, and like them they should keep on the alert as well as keep cool.

The Weapon of Starvation.

They were all at the front in this war especially those resident at the sea-side, for all would play their part. They could not tell when or where the blow would fall, but they would be better prepared to meet it if all organisations such as theirs were waiting to be of assistance, for the enemy had the other ways of fighting besides shot and shell – there was the weapon of starvation from that more would suffer than shot and shell. Indeed, he would make this one prophecy – more would die from starvation and anguish, through the rash conduct of the Kaiser than through wounds received in the battle. Therefore, it was their duty to parry the blows that would fall by bringing into use their great and yet minute organisation which would deal promptly and adequately with this distress. But let them lessen the likelihood of distress by employing as far as they could those without money, and in that connexion he might urge any present who were employers to go almost to the point of danger with regard to their banking balances before resolving to close down their workshop.

No Peace Theories Until...

Sir Harry proceeded to speak reproachfully of those employers who "seemed to have less of the milk of human kindness than others", and on the other hand to laud those theatre managers who despite the discouraging signs were keeping open their engagements and rising to the inconvenience of the time. He begged of them in conclusion to go out of their way to find employment for the work people, to resolve for instance, to have their houses done up to a far more expensive extent than strictly necessary because he warned them they would not be able to put their peace theories into practice until "Germany gone Mad" had been entirely beaten, and the spirit of militarism had been put down for good. To Prussian tendencies he preferred to attribute this blame for this inexcusable War. No parallel could be recalled to the speeches of the German Emperor and his Minister of State. (Applause.)

Speeches by Miss Urlin and Mr Keighley.

Miss Urlin (Hon. Secretary of the Rustington branch) followed with a very thoughtful paper. This war was justified as far as they were concerned because they were fighting for their existence as a nation. Yet war was a horrible thing, and so it was their place as women to bring into the time a spirit of peace and love. They all esteemed it their duty to do something for the need at the front. Let them all pull together, let all shoulders be at the wheel, now was their opportunity to demonstrate their worthiness for the vote. She hoped they would all strive to bring about peace very quickly. They should remember that reason, love and moral power did not lose in the long run.

Mr TD Keighley, in the course of a brief speech said that at such a crisis as the present women were able to prove their worth, for their vision was ten times clearer than that of men. Men often allowed passion to blind them, for their blood flowed faster and sometimes prevented them from being ruled by reason. In the present war, right would triumph. He proposed a vote of thanks to Lady Parry, Sir Harry Johnston and Miss Urlin.

Every German not an Enemy.

This was seconded with considerable will by Mr Israel Zangwill, who urged them not to regard every German as an enemy. What quarrel could they have with the millions of harmless Fraus and good natured Teutons? No, their quarrel was with the German Emperor and his Prussian advisers and professors, through whom the Germans had contracted swollen heads. As soon as Germany was no longer ridden by the military caste the better. Then the spirit of brotherhood and good nature would have a chance.

The vote was carried with acclamation, but, in reply, Sir Harry expressed his hope that among other things, the war would remove from among us "vote of thanks".

Mrs Russell closed the gathering by mentioning that *The Observer* had already published an intimation, which had been a great help to them, as to the proposals of the National Union of Women's Suffrage Societies. Their committee had met and they were mapping out a programme for relief purposes.

The company then adjourned to the house where tea was served.' (*Chichester Observer and West Sussex Recorder*, 1914.)

Meetings were held quite often both during and after the war. One of these meetings was held in The Lecture Hall in Littlehampton where Mrs Henry Fawcett (as it was advertised) was to give an address.

Fig. 71 Lady Maude Parry leading a march in Littlehampton.

In Littlehampton, suffragettes would come down to stay at the Green Lady Hostel (now called Mewsbrook House) in East Street. Most of the suffragettes took it upon themselves to wear green suits and white blouses or green dresses with special jewellery designed for them to wear, particularly emeralds and seed pearls set in gold. Hence, the name "Green Lady". The locals still call the footpath that runs from East Street to Cornwall Road "The Green Lady". This property had been purchased by Lily Montagu CBE and Mrs Emmeline Pethick-Lawrence as a seaside holiday house for female factory workers and established by Mary Neal and Emmeline (founders of the Esperence Girls' Club) in 1900.

During 1883, the year following Rhoda's death, Sir Hubert Parry had a very productive year, rich in achievement and recognition. Not only did he write *The Glories of our Blood and State*, as mentioned in a previous chapter, but also was offered on New Year's Day the post of Professorship of Musical History at the Royal College of Music, opened by the Prince of Wales on May 7th and conferred on him the honorary degree of Doctor of Music. He also had written other symphonies including the music to the *Birds of Aristophanes* that had great success at Cambridge. Sir Hubert Parry had stayed with Millicent and Sir Henry Fawcett during this period at Cambridge. (Graves, 1926.)

Dame Ethyl Smyth had also become very interested in women's suffrage following Rhoda's death, despite having shown no real interest when she had first met Rhoda. Rhoda's passion for the cause must have rubbed off on the composer. Dame Ethyl Smyth had sided with the suffragettes led by Emmeline Pankhurst (who as I stated in an earlier chapter that the first meeting Emmeline, then aged 15, attended was for a speech given by Rhoda Garrett, amongst others) and these two women were to become the greatest of friends, and during 1910 she wrote the *March of the Women* (see Fig. 72), which became the Women's Social and Political Union (WSPU) battle hymn.

Whilst the WSPU leader was staying at Coign on Hook Heath near Woking, Surrey, as a guest of Dame Ethel Smyth, her host taught her how to throw a stone by aiming her missile at the largest fir tree. 'One has heard of people failing to hit a haystack,' remembered Ethel, 'what followed was rather on those lines. I imagine Mrs Pankhurst had not played ball games in her youth, and the first stone flew backwards out of her hand, narrowly missing my dog.' With each failed attempt, Emmeline assumed a more and more ferocious expression until a loud thud proclaimed success and a "smile of such beatitude" stole across her face that Ethel collapsed in laughter amongst the heather. Emmeline was not amused. (Smyth, 1933.)

During 1912, Emmeline Pankhurst was immediately arrested on 1st March for smashing windows at 10 Downing Street along with over 100 other women for the breaking of around four hundred shop windows. On 4th March, a further 96 arrests were made, including Dame Ethel Smyth for smashing the window of an anti-suffrage politician in Downing Street and Elizabeth Garrett Anderson's daughter, Dr Louisa Garrett Anderson.

Emmeline was recuperating at Dame Ethel's home in Hook Heath, near Woking, Surrey, following her hunger strike, when she was to be re-arrested under the infamous "Cat and Mouse" Act enacted by the government of the time on 26th May 1913.

Fig. 72 *The March of the Women* by Dame Ethel Smyth.

Elizabeth Garrett Anderson's activities on behalf of the movement increased following the death of her husband Skelton in 1907. She had joined the WSPU but, in late 1911, Elizabeth wrote to Emmeline Pankhurst withdrawing her membership because of the increase in their militant activities. This had followed a letter from Millicent to her in December 1911 stating that '...We have the best chance of Women's Suffrage next session that we have ever had, by far, if it is not destroyed by disgusting masses of people by revolutionary violence.' Elizabeth agreed with her sister saying, 'I am quite with you with the WSPU. I think they are quite wrong.' However, as we've seen above, her daughter Louisa Garrett Anderson joined in with the militant tactics. This upset Millicent; she wrote to Elizabeth saying, 'I am in hopes she will take her punishment wisely, that the enforced solitude will help her to see more in focus than she always does.' (Taylor and Taylor BEM, 2015.)

I often wonder which side of the divide Rhoda would have taken. I think if she had still been alive during these turbulent times, she would have had the reputation of their firm R & A Garrett to think about, but given her strength of personality, I reckon she would have taken the more militant approach.

Agnes had continued to run the business successfully for many years, including the redecoration of Elizabeth's home in Aldeburgh in 1884 and submitting and winning a tender for the New Hospital for Women; Millicent and Philippa came to live with her at 2 Gower Street following Henry Fawcett's death in 1884.

Agnes was to be heavily involved in another successful adventure, of which I'm sure Rhoda would have discussed the possibilities with her cousins. Emily Davies had mooted the idea in an article, in February 1863, in the *English Women's Journal* called "Modern Housebuilding", which recommended flat-living for women. Agnes was to become one of the founding directors of a new company in 1880 called "The Ladies' Residential Chambers Limited", along with James Beale, John Westlake and Christiana Herringham, with Rev Giles Pilcher as chairman. (Crawford, 2002.)

One hundred shares of £10 each were on offer; some of these shares were taken up by Elizabeth Garrett Anderson, Millicent Fawcett, Agnes Garrett and James Beale's wife Margaret. (They were the couple who moved to Standen, which is now owned by the National Trust, housing furniture designed by R & A Garrett.)

They were proposing to erect a block of chambers on a site owned by the Bedford Estate, in Chenies Street, off Gower Street. These were subsequently built and opened by Millicent Fawcett on 20th May 1889.

The chambers were intended for educated women earning their own living, for example, teachers, artists, doctors etc. The building housed many flats with two, three or four rooms and a commercial dining room and kitchen on the ground floor.

Agnes was a driving force for the enterprise that enabled professional women to live in the comfort of a well-managed home for 43 years. She attended her last director's meeting in March 1931.

The Garrett connection with 2 Gower Street continued until 1938 when, three years after Agnes's death, Philippa gave up the tenancy.

However, it was Agnes's younger sister Millicent who was to be the most prominent of the sisters in the women's suffrage movement. Millicent would have learned a lot from her older cousin Rhoda through both her guidance and her brilliant speeches.

Millicent was to become the president of the National Union of Women's Suffrage Societies (NUWSS) from 1897 until 1918, when the vote was secured for women. She also co-founded Newnham College in Cambridge.

Henry and Millicent's daughter, Philippa, was educated at Newnham College and, like most of the Garretts, turned out to be exceptionally talented. In 1890, she became the first woman to come top in the Cambridge Mathematical Tripos exams, receiving 13% more than the next highest. However, she did not receive the title of senior wrangler as only men were allowed this title. Coming amidst the women's suffrage movement the result gathered huge international coverage. The lead story in *The Telegraph* the following day said, 'Once again has woman demonstrated her superiority in the face of incredulous and unsympathetic world... And now the trench has been carried by Amazonian assault, and the whole citadel of learning lies open and defenceless before the victorious students of Newnham and Girton [founded by Emily Davies]. There is no longer any field of learning in which the lady student does not excel.' (Taylor and Taylor BEM, 2015.)

Philippa and her mother were to later set up the education system in the Transvaal following the Boer War. Millicent had been asked, by the British government, in August 1901, to head a committee of British women to investigate Emily Hobhouse's (a member of the NUWSS) complaints about the conditions in the concentration camps in South Africa during the Anglo-Boer War. The Fawcett Commission reported that 27,927 Boers had died of starvation, disease and exposure in the concentration camps, following Kitchener's "Scorched Earth" policy, which involved the poisoning of wells, salting of fields and the systematic burning of homesteads and livestock. Civilians were then moved by force to the concentration camps. The report said that about a quarter of all Boers inmates, mostly children, had died. (Taylor and Taylor BEM, 2015.)

A landmark date for the women's suffrage movement finally came on 6th February 1918 when The Representation of the People Act was passed; this allowed women over the age of 30, provided they were married to a property owner to vote and to also allow all men over the age of 21 and men in the armed forces over the age of 19.

It was following this Act that the Rustington connection with the Garrett family was to once again come to the fore again. On 13th March 1918, Sir Hubert Parry attended the concert held at the Albert Hall organised to celebrate the final stage of the Votes for Women campaign for which he'd taken charge of the music, and on 15th March Millicent Fawcett wrote to him saying, '...The music said for us what no words could say, and it was an added delight that you were in charge of it all, with memories going back to Rhoda and Agnes in their young days and of Harry [Henry Fawcett] with all his chivalries and enthusiasms. The Council passed a special vote of thanks to you, the Bach Choir and the Orchestra yesterday, but this is a little personal line. Your "Jerusalem" ought to be made the Women Voters' Hymn...'

Mrs Fawcett alluded to his setting of Blake's poem, which ends with the memorable words:

'I will not cease from mental fight,

Nor shall my sword sleep in my hand,

Till we have built Jerusalem

In England's green and pleasant land.'

Sir Hubert Parry replied to her letter on 18th March, saying, '...a glorious occasion for you and everyone concerned. Quite thrilling. I thought myself very lucky to be allowed to take part in it.' He recollected with affection from his early married life when Agnes and Rhoda were neighbours and intimates back in the 1870s and early 1880s when in Rustington, when neighbours were few, and mentions of their wonderful kindness and helpfulness in any domestic difficulty abound in his early diaries. There is always a caress in his reference to them and their way of life and outlook. The letter to Mrs Fawcett ends with an acknowledgement:

'Your choice of the *Leonara* overture was an inspiration! How it did fit! I confess I was very anxious about the music. It was such a responsibility. But it seemed to come out all right, and the performers put their backs into it with a will. Thank you for what you say about the "Jerusalem" song. I wish indeed it might become the Women Voters' hymn, as you suggest. People seem to enjoy singing it. And having the vote ought to diffuse a good deal of joy too. So they would combine happily. A thousand thanks for being so kind. Love to Agnes, please.' (Graves, 1926.)

The following month Millicent Fawcett came down to speak in Littlehampton and the event was recorded in a local magazine as follows:

'It should be of interest to readers of *Scribble* to learn that Mrs Henry Fawcett, President of the National Union of Women's Suffrage, in commemoration of the passing of the Women's Suffrage Bill, was chief speaker on April 12th at Littlehampton. Mrs Fawcett was supported by Sir C Hubert H Parry, Bart., Lady Maud Parry being in the chair. That the president of the NUWSS should consent to speak in this locality, after refusing over 100 requests to speak elsewhere, is both a compliment to her local supporters and also a token of the memory of old ties with Rustington, where as long ago as 40 years, she and her husband the late Postmaster General, were wont to stay, and where, with a small coterie of relations and friends, women's suffrage was discussed, and a petition for it was signed by a large proportion of Rustington people. It has been said that Rustington was the cradle of women's suffrage.

An anti-militant, Mrs Fawcett has worked with dignity, fidelity, and an infinite patience for the cause which has been for so long the ambition of thousands of thinking men and women.

The lecture hall was filled with an enthusiastic audience, and an interesting message was received from Sir Harry Johnston, who regretted his inability to be present, but who said that he was only just recovering from a "whiff" of mustard gas inhaled near the German lines.

"We look now," he said, "to the men and women of the masses to save this country and all the best things that this great Empire stands for, to save us from mismanagement of the educated upper classes, and to save us from the general effects all round of a most inadequate education in all things that really matter. To save us from the waste and plunder that has hitherto characterised our methods of government." We have referred to other items, less serious, in our editorial.' (Hollis, April 1918.)

The editorial referred to above seems to epitomise the sort of journalism that accompanied the cause throughout the period of campaigning and is quoted below:

'In another column of this issue we refer to the meeting at Littlehampton on April 12th. It was indeed a pleasure to listen to Mrs Henry Fawcett, and Lady Maud Parry made an excellent Chairwoman, although it might have been better if she had insisted on a time limit.

Sir Hubert gave us about an hour of most interesting reminiscences, ranging from ladies' hats to mustard plasters, with a little sea bathing thrown in.

Three questions to Mrs Fawcett elicited the following facts, that:

1. Suffragettes intend to become members of Parliament.
2. They do not at present intend to run independent candidates.
3. When women have equal voting powers with men they will have a large majority of votes.

Unless, therefore, we follow the Chinese system with girl babies, the House of Commons in years to come will be run by women.

If this should happen, we anticipate that Westminster Abbey will have to be given over to Members' babies and their nurses. Specials would then indeed be necessary to regulate the perambulator traffic.

We certainly believe, as has been proved, that women can do a lot to help government of the country both in parochial and parliamentary affairs, but when it comes to having unequal voting powers of the country behind them which can enforce "petticoat government", man would then become a "mere thing". As, in the beginning, women was sent into the world to be a "helpmeet" to man, and it is told to us in Genesis that man should rule over woman, they will never be able to exercise their voting powers to carry all before them.' (Hollis, Women's

Suffrage in Editorial, April 1918.)

Sadly, the Garrett's great friend Sir Hubert Parry died later that year on 7th October 1918.

So, finally all the hard campaigning by Rhoda and other pioneers came to fruition and it was Rhoda's cousin Millicent Fawcett who was to be instrumental in gaining the vote for six million British women over the age of 30.

Fig. 73

Extract from Parry's original manuscript of *Jerusalem* (1916).

Ray Strachey (born Rachel Pearsall Conn Costelloe) was born five years after Rhoda died; she became a great friend of Millicent, Philippa and Agnes and is famously pictured in a car together celebrating the Equal Franchise Act, 1928. Ray Strachey became a writer and a feminist politician. She knew very well Rhoda's reputation as a speaker and she wrote of Rhoda saying, '...in every way a brilliant young woman, easily the most eloquent and convincing of all the early speakers, and popular wherever she went.' (Strachey, 1931.)

Agnes and Millicent were to spend their time in retirement travelling and it was on one of these occasions, ironically whilst in Jerusalem, in 1928, when they were 85 and 83 respectively that they were to hear that the Bill to give women the vote on the same terms as men had been passed. The two sisters joined hands and danced around the room they were staying in. (Bentwich and Bentwich, 1965.)

Dame Millicent Fawcett died the following year on 5th August 1929, but unlike Rhoda at least she was able to see her dreams realised. Dame Millicent's legacy lives on through the women's charity, The Fawcett Society. On 12th March 1932, a memorial service was held for the unveiling of a memorial to Dame Millicent Fawcett; they had added her to the one for Henry Fawcett. This memorial can still be seen in Westminster Abbey.

However, a more individual and fitting tribute is to happen in 2018, as on 20th September 2017, a statue designed by the Turner Prize-winning artist Gillian Wearing of Dame Millicent Fawcett has been given planning permission to be built in Parliament Square alongside Sir Winston Churchill and Nelson Mandela. It will portray Dame Millicent Fawcett holding a placard reading: "Courage calls to courage everywhere." This was an extract from a speech that she gave following the death in 1913 of campaigner Emily Davison at the Epsom Derby. The bronze casting will be unveiled in 2018 to coincide with the centenary of women winning the right to vote. It will be the first statue of a woman in Parliament Square.

In conclusion, I believe Rhoda Garrett was a most remarkable person, one of those rare people who commanded respect from everyone, even her opponents. To have two pieces of music dedicated to her from different composers shows how truly remarkable she was. Rhoda had a presence about her that when she was in the room you only had eyes for her. Rhoda truly was one in a million!

Appendix 1

CERTIFIED COPY OF AN ENTRY OF BIRTH

GIVEN AT THE GENERAL REGISTER OFFICE

Application Number 7629909-1

REGISTRATION DISTRICT BAKEWELL UNION

1841 BIRTH in the Sub-district of Mattock in the County of Derby

No.	When and where born	Name, if any	Sex	Name and surname of father	Name, surname and maiden surname of mother	Occupation of father	Signature, description and residence of informant	When registered	Signature of registrar	Name entered after registration
1	2	3	4	5	6	7	8	9	10	
232	Twenty eighth of [illegible] 1841 at Elton	Rhoda	Girl	John Fisher Garratt	Elizabeth Henry Garratt formerly [illegible]	Clerk	Eliz. Henry Garratt Mother Elton	Twenty eighth of April 1841	William Stafford Registrar	

CERTIFIED to be a true copy of an entry in the certified copy of a Register of Births in the District above mentioned.

Given at the GENERAL REGISTER OFFICE, under the Seal of the said Office, the 13th day of September 2016

BXCG 973655

CAUTION: THERE ARE OFFENCES RELATING TO FALSIFYING OR ALTERING A CERTIFICATE AND USING OR POSSESSING A FALSE CERTIFICATE ©CROWN COPYRIGHT

WARNING: A CERTIFICATE IS NOT EVIDENCE OF IDENTITY.

GENERAL REGISTER OFFICE ENGLAND

JBF

Copy of Rhoda's Birth Certificate.

Appendix 2

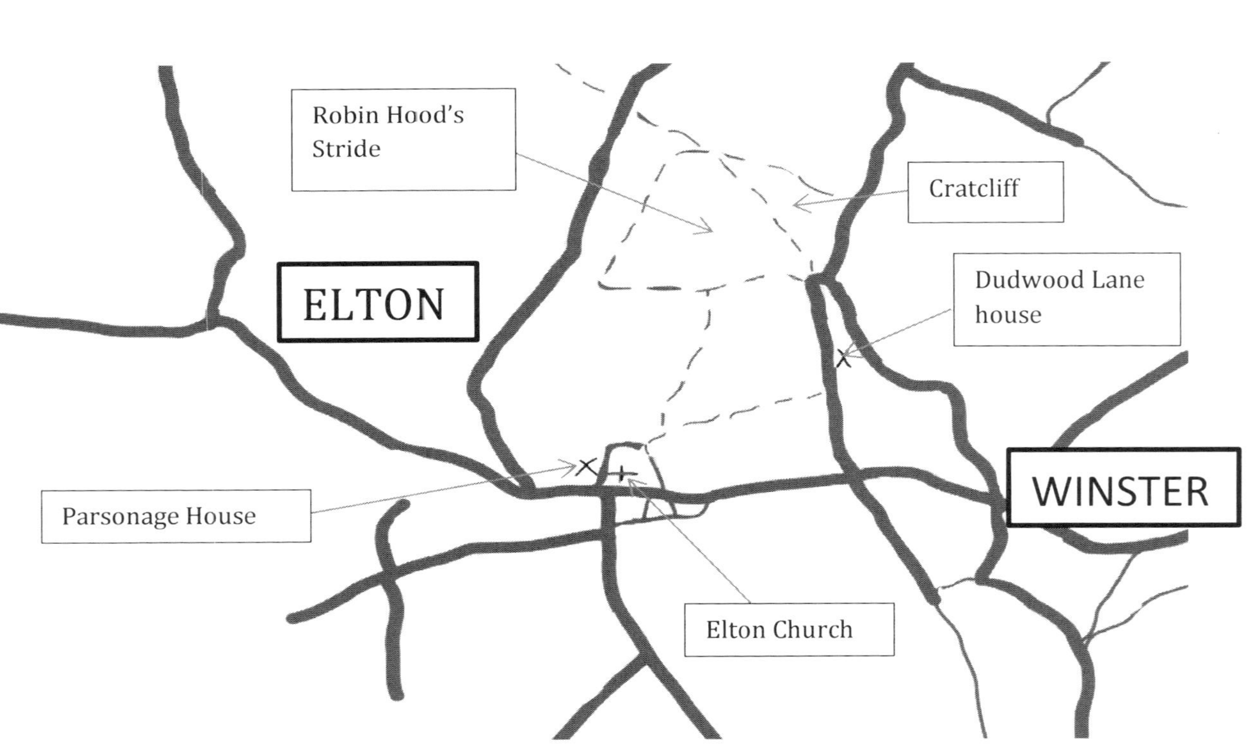

Map of Elton showing Rhoda's birthplace, "Parsonage House".

Appendix 3

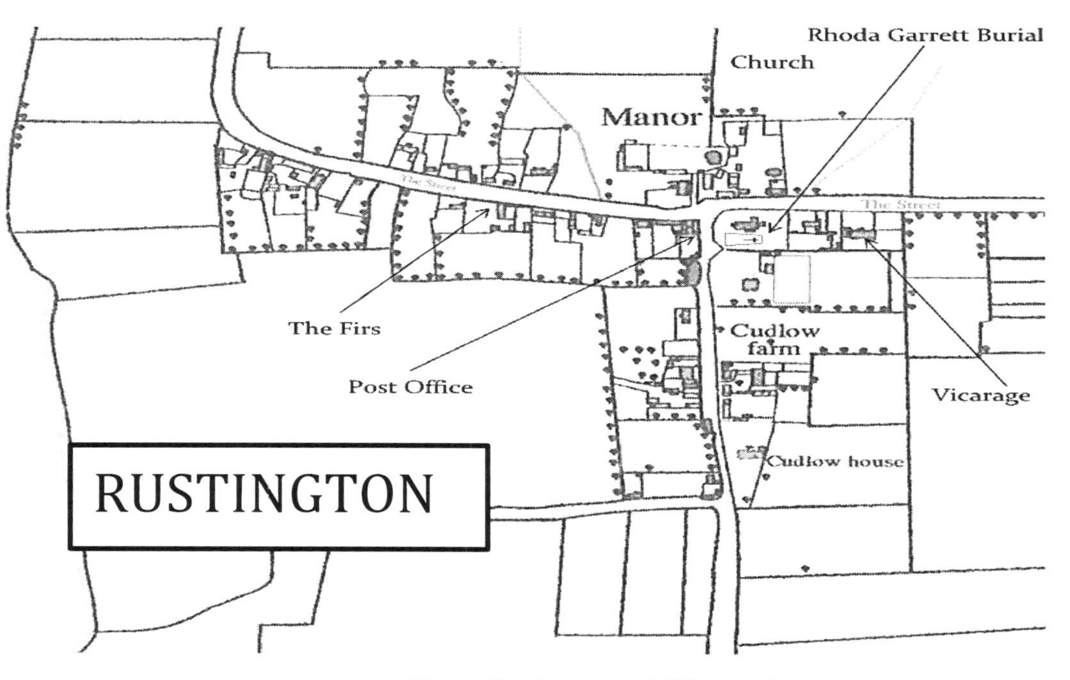

Rustington (Central) – Location of "The Firs".

Appendix 4

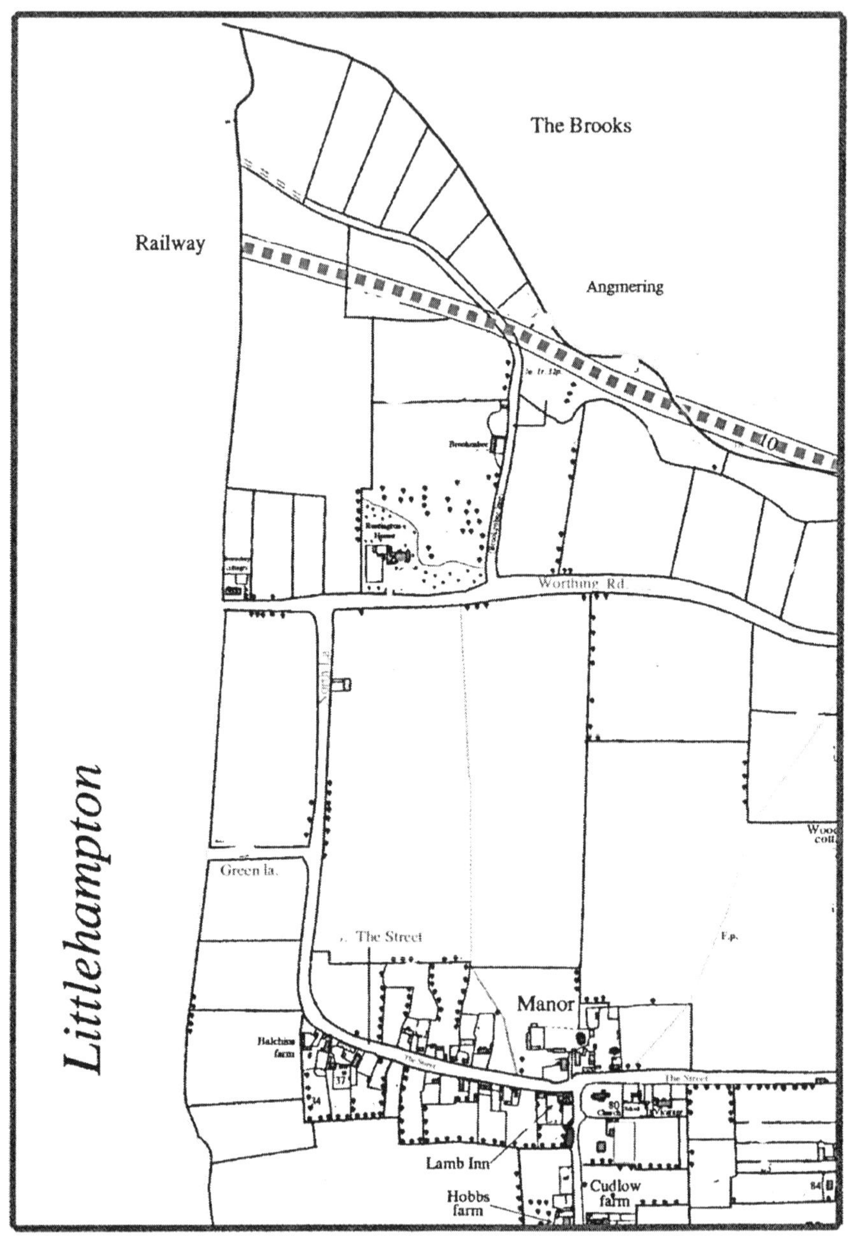

Rustington (North West).

Appendix 5

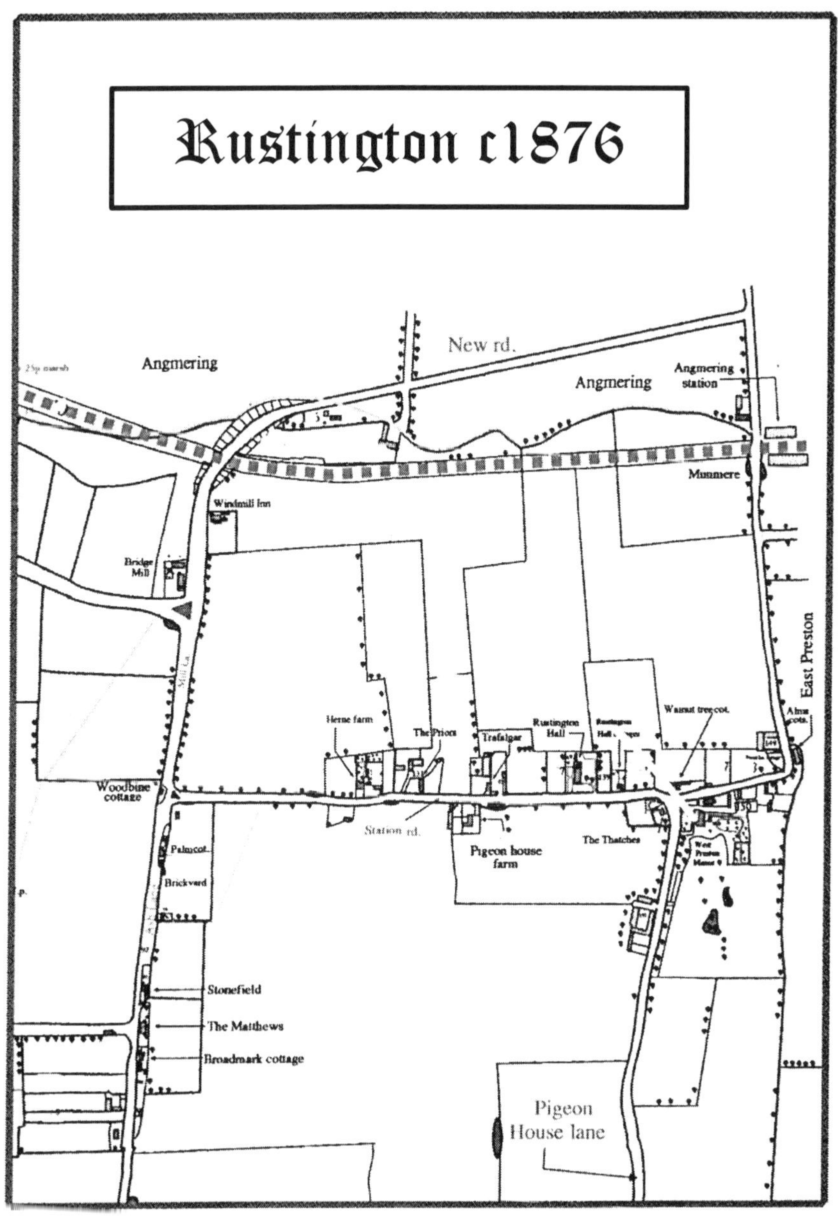

Rustington (North East).

Appendix 6

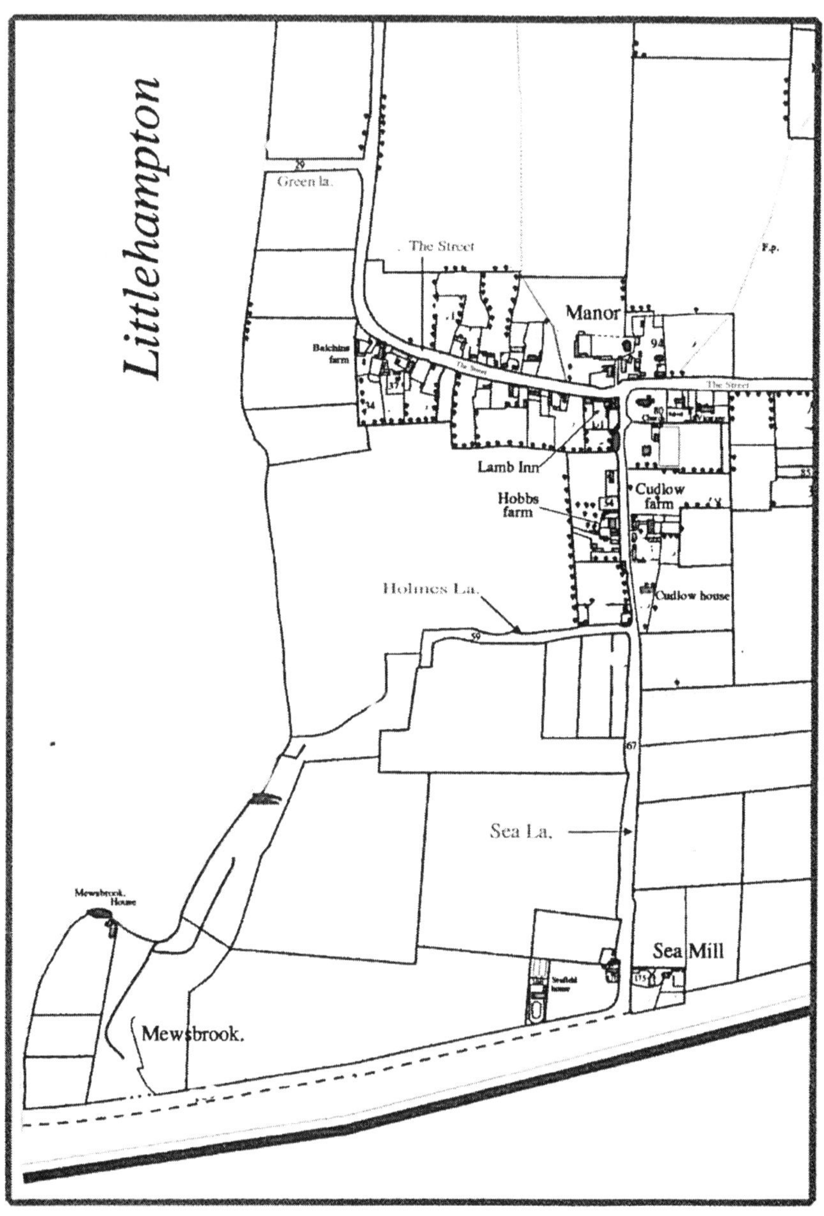

Rustington (South West).

Appendix 7

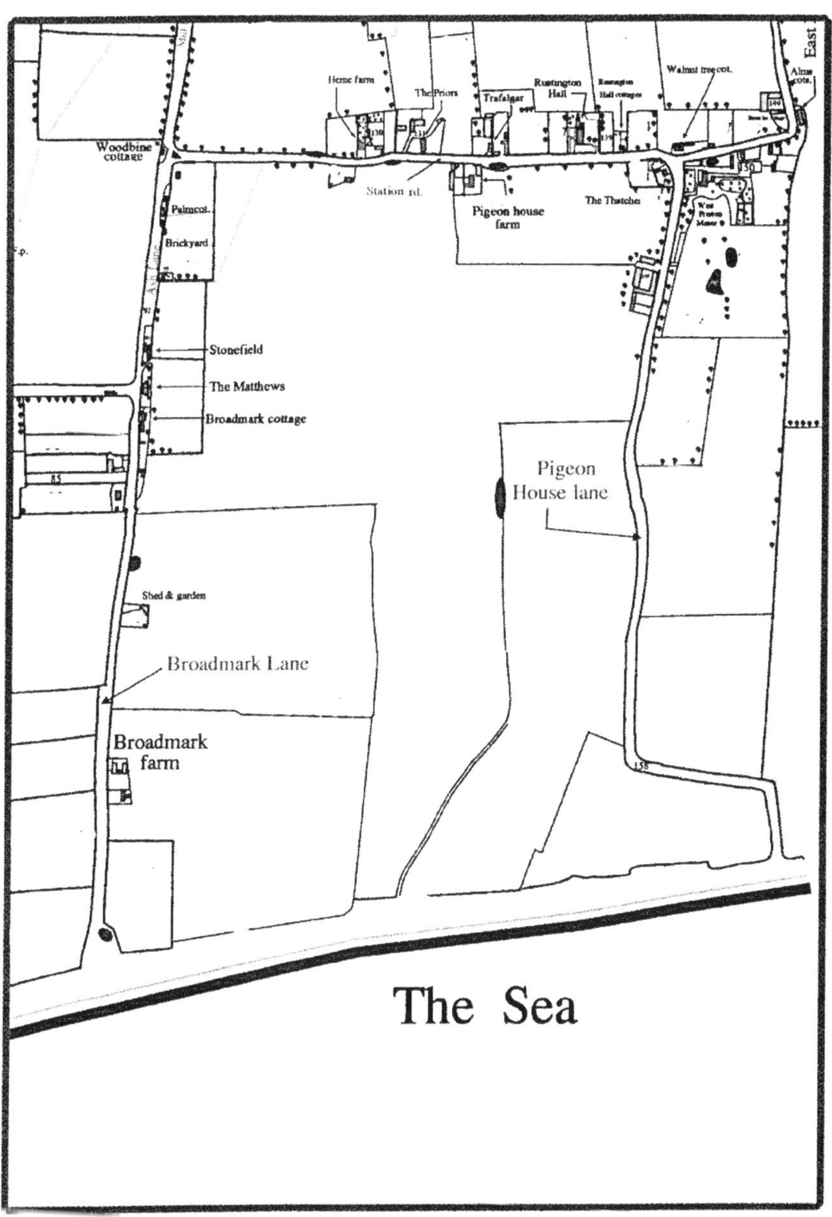

Rustington (South East).

Appendix 8

CERTIFIED COPY OF AN ENTRY OF DEATH

GIVEN AT THE GENERAL REGISTER OFFICE

Application Number 6021388-1

REGISTRATION DISTRICT ST GILES

1882 DEATH in the Sub-district of St Giles North in the County of Middlesex

Columns:- 1		2	3	4	5	6	7	8	9
No.	When and where died	Name and surname	Sex	Age	Occupation	Cause of death	Signature, description and residence of informant	When registered	Signature of registrar
495	Twenty second November 1882 2 Gower Street	Rhoda Garrett	Female	40 years	[illegible] Daughter of John Fisher Garrett (deceased) Rector of Elton Derbyshire	Typhoid Fever 23 days Bronchitis 12 days Certified by E. G. Anderson M.D. L.S.A. Lond	Mary Jardine Present at Death 2 Gower Street	Twenty third November 1882	W. B. Peach Registrar

CERTIFIED to be a true copy of an entry in the certified copy of a Register of Deaths in the District above mentioned.

Given at the GENERAL REGISTER OFFICE, under the Seal of the said Office, the 5th day of November 2014

DYD 775368

See note overleaf

CAUTION: THERE ARE OFFENCES RELATING TO FALSIFYING OR ALTERING A CERTIFICATE AND USING OR POSSESSING A FALSE CERTIFICATE ©CROWN COPYRIGHT

WARNING: A CERTIFICATE IS NOT EVIDENCE OF IDENTITY.

GENERAL REGISTER OFFICE ENGLAND

Copy of Rhoda's Death Certificate.

Acknowledgements

I am most grateful to all the staff at the various archives and libraries that I have visited in the course of my research into this book.

It has been a most pleasurable experience visiting the many places and people in order to complete this work, including visits to Elton and the surrounding areas in Derbyshire; Ventnor on the Isle of Wight; both Shulbrede Priory and Rustington in West Sussex; various trips to London and finally Snape Maltings, Aldeburgh and Leiston in Suffolk. I cannot go on further here without mentioning the friendliness and hospitality of "The Butchers Arms" in Knodishall where I spent a couple nights. Thank you.

I would like to especially thank the following people for the help and information provided to me. The National Trust, Standen (who allowed me access out of hours to view and photograph items of Garrett furniture; Dr Caroline Adams for obtaining the recipe for the Lardy Cakes and to Martin Hayes for his help in this matter and general encouragement; Sue Sula, Rustington Past and Present and Rich Pegrum for the Lardy Cake recipe used by RJ Pegrum & Son in Rustington in more recent times; The Long Shop Museum in Leiston for putting me in touch with some of the Garrett descendants and the information boards on Elizabeth Garrett Anderson on the 100th anniversary of her death; the cast of *A Woman of Purpose – The Life and Times of Elizabeth Garrett Anderson*, a new play by Suzanne Hawkes (Black and White Productions) who produced a fantastic and most informative performance as a promenade play around the town of Aldeburgh, including Alde House, which had been built to Elizabeth, Agnes and Millicent's father, Newson Garrett's own design; I'd especially like to thank Suzanne Hawkes who I had a long chat with on the Garrett family; Kate Ponsonby and Ian Russell for allowing me access to Sir Hubert Parry, Lady Maude Parry and their daughter Dolly's diaries, which have been most useful and for lending me copies of the two volumes of *Sir Hubert Parry*, written by CL Graves and the original sheet music of *The Glories of our Blood and State*; however, I'd like to particularly give tribute to the Late Laura Ponsonby of Shulbrede Priory for the copies of the only two known letters written by Rhoda Garrett still in existence and the unpublished work, written and illustrated by Lady Maude Parry as a tribute to Rhoda (as seen in the introduction) and if it hadn't been for Laura I most probably wouldn't have been writing this book; The Elton Local History Group and specifically Lynn Burnet for her hospitality and for showing my late wife Sue and I around Rhoda's birthplace "Parsonage House" (The Old Rectory) along with a guided tour of Elton Church; Elizabeth Crawford for all her help and encouragement in writing this book and allowing me to use extracts from her books and for contacting members of the wider Garrett family to enable me to use further photographs; Ria Mills at "The Firs" as I shall always know it, for her kind hospitality and showing me around Rhoda's house!

Finally on this front I'd like to give my heartfelt thanks to my Mum and Dad, the local historians of Rustington (Bev and Mary Taylor BEM). Dad for his maps and his comprehensive records of the censuses/parish records etc., which have been an invaluable source of information, jointly for the postcards and photographs from their collection and to Mum for her in-depth knowledge of the village, her encouragement, proof reading on a regular basis throughout. If it wasn't for Mum I certainly wouldn't have ever written a book!

I'd also like to offer my thanks to Graham Cook and his team at Writersworld for making the whole process of publishing my book so straightforward. I'd like to thank Jag Lall for the superb front and back cover design and to Ian Large for all his help with the editing and indexing.

There are certain people without whom this book would not have been possible, particularly in what has turned out to be such a devastating year on a personal front for me and my family. At the end of December 2016, my darling wife Sue was diagnosed with Mesothelioma (The Asbestos Cancer) having worked for the NHS all her life and despite her amazing courage and continuous organisation throughout, which included being on top form for my daughter Bethany's wedding to Liam in April (where if you didn't know you would certainly not have guessed how ill she was), lost her battle on 26th June 2017. I'd like to thank everyone at St Barnabas Hospice for their care and kindness throughout, to Hannah Binstead for listening when I needed somebody to talk to not long after Sue was diagnosed and to all my friends and family in what has been a most difficult period and for spurring me on to finish the book.

Finally, I'd like to thank my family; my brother-in law Paul, his wife Florence, and their children Emily and James; a special thank you to my nephew Paul and his wife Jenny for their help and support, especially during those difficult days at the end of June; my brother Andrew and his wife Nicky who have been constantly there for us and their children, Jenny, twins Avalon and Rupert and identical twins Robyn and Tawney; not forgetting my Mum and Dad for all their love and help; and finally, with all my love to my daughter Bethany (Beth) and her husband Liam, my son Iain who helped me with a couple of the maps in the appendices, which needed adjusting, and to Edward (Ed) for having to put up with the constant talk about Rhoda and the research material which has amassed around our house!

I would like to dedicate this book to my late wife Sue

(1962-2017)

Fig. 74 Sue at Robin Hood's Stride, Elton in August 2016.

Picture Acknowledgements

Author's collection: Front cover, 8 (courtesy of Shulbrede Priory), 11, 13, 15, 16, 17, 20, 21, 23, 24, 38, 46, 49, 50, 60, 65, 67, 97, 100-1 (the last 3 pages from R & A Garrett, *House Decoration*), 102, 110, 113 (from R Strachey, Women's Suffrage and Women's Service), 120, 128, 133 (from Dame Ethel Smyth, *Impressions that Remained*), 135, 141, 143 (courtesy of Shulbrede Priory), 144, 152, 155, 165, 171 (courtesy of Shulbrede Priory), 185

Bev and Mary Taylor B.E.M.: 63, 112-9, 123-6, 142, 163

The Illustrated London News: 25, 59, 84

Wanganui Chronicle: 28

Hew Stevenson: 44

The Cabinet Maker: 136

Mr Caswall Smith (1895) from the book *Edmund Garrett: A Memoir* by ET Cook: 151

Pauline Hadlow for the photo of John and Amy Badley: 154

Bibliography

Archival Sources

Anderson Family Papers, Suffolk Record Office, Ipswich.

Bev and Mary Taylor B.E.M. Parish of Rustington History Archives including maps.

Shulbrede Priory: Diaries of Sir Hubert and Lady Maude Parry; Letters from Rhoda Garrett to Lady Maude Parry; Letters from Agnes Garrett and Fydell Edmund Garrett to Lady Maude.

Society for the Protection of Ancient Buildings: The Society's Papers; Papers of Thackaray Turner.

The British Newspaper Archive.

The Long Room Museum at Leiston.

UK Census collection.

Women's Library: Haweis Papers; microfilm of the Millicent Garrett Fawcett Papers; Autograph Collection.

Journals

Bedales Magazine

The Cabinet Maker and Art Furnisher

The House Furnisher and Decorator

Journal of Decorative Art and British Decorator

Macmillan's Magazine

Unpublished Typescripts

Parry, Lady Maude, *Pen and Ink Sketches 'Rhoda Garrett'*.

Books and online sources

Bartley, P. (2002). *Emmeline Pankhurst*. 1st ed. Abingdon: Routledge, p.22.

Bates, T. (2017). *Elton | Elton Village | Elton Guide | Peak District | Derbyshire*. [online] Peakdistrictonline.co.uk. Available at: http://www.peakdistrictonline.co.uk/elton-c125.html [Accessed 31 May 2016].

Belich, J. (2010) *I Shall Not Die: Titokowaru's War, 1868-1869*. 2nd ed. Wellington, New Zealand: Bridget Williams Books, pp.199-216.

Bentwich, N. and Bentwich, H. (1965). *Mandate Memories, 1918-1948.* 1st ed. New York: Schocken Books, p.115.

Burnet, L. (2016). *Climate in the 19th Century.* [online] Sites.google.com. Available at: https://sites.google.com/a/eltonvillage.com/elton-village-local-history/index/environment/climate [Accessed 2 Sep. 2016].

Burnet, L. (2016). *Sign in - Google Accounts.* [online] Sites.google.com. Available at: https://sites.google.com/a/eltonvillage.com/elton-village-local-history/index/people/john-fisher-garrett [Accessed 31 Aug. 2016].

Burnet, L. (2010). *Rectors Remembered.* 1st ed. Elton: Elton Local History Group, p.3.

Chichester Express and West Sussex Journal (1867). Marriage of Mr Henry Fawcett. p.4.

Chichester Observer and West Sussex Recorder (1914). Suffragists and the War. p.3.

Conway, M. (1904). *Autobiography: Memories and Experiences of Moncure Daniel Conway Vol. 1.* 1st ed. Boston and New York: Houghton, Mifflin and Company, pp.450-451.

Conway, M. (1882). *Travels in South Kensington with Notes on Decorative Art and Architecture in England.* 1st ed. Trubner, p.169.

Cook, E. (1909). *Edmund Garrett. A Memoir.* 1st ed. Edward Arnold: London.

Crawford, E. (2002). *Enterprising Women – The Garretts and their Circle.* London: Francis Boutle Publishers.

Crawford, E. (1999). *The Women's Suffrage Movement in Britain: A Reference Guide 1866-1928.* 1st ed. London: UCL Press.

Dundee Courier (1882). Rhoda and Agnes Garrett. p.7.

Eades, G. (2015). *The Royal National Hospital for Chest Diseases.* [online] iowhospitals. Available at: http://connect.iow.nhs.uk/Uploads/HealingArts/News_and_events/Ventnor%20A%20Victorian%20Hospital%20Web%20Sept%2015%20Final_2015-10-07_13-13-50-549.pdf [Accessed 13 Nov. 2016].

Fawcett, M. (1924). *What I Remember.* 1st ed. London: T Fisher Unwin, pp.48-54.

Fawcett, M. (1912). *Women's Suffrage.* 1st ed. Edinburgh; London: T.C. & E.C. Jack.

Garrett Anderson, L. (1939). *Elizabeth Garrett Anderson 1836-1917.* 1st ed. London: Faber and Faber.

Garrett, R. (1916). The Old Kai Iwi Troop. *Wanganui Chronicle*, p.3.

Garrett, R & A (1877). *Suggestions for House Decoration in Painting, Woodwork and Furniture*. 2nd ed. London: Macmillan and Co.

Garrett, R. (1872). *Electoral Disabilities of Women*. [Pamphlet printed by the Telegraph Office, Cheltenham]. University of Bristol Library Special Collections, Feminist Collection South: Ellen Malos Archive: History of the Women's Movement 1869-2001. Bristol.

Graves, C. (1926). *Hubert Parry: His Life and Works Vol.1*. 1st ed. London: Macmillan and Co, p.206.

Hughes, G. (2017). *The Foods of England – Winster Wakes Cake*. [online] Foodsofengland.co.uk. Available at: http://www.foodsofengland.co.uk/WinsterWakesCake.htm [Accessed 28 Sep. 2017].

Illustrated London News (1851). The Great Exhibition. p.587.

London Evening Standard (1873). The Taunton Election. p.5.

London Evening Standard (1873). The Plain Truth About Taunton. p.6.

Morning Post (1873). Taunton. p.5.

New Zealand Herald (1883). To Members of Mr. Bryce's Old Kai Iwi Troop of Cavalry. p.1.

North Devon Journal (1874). London Gossip. p.6.

Pugh, M. (1980). *Women's Suffrage in Britain, 1867-1928*. 1st ed. London: The Historical Associaton.

Ryalls, C. (1877). *Transactions of the National Association for the Promotion of Social Science*. 1st ed. London: Longmans, Green, and Co., pp.863-865.

Samuelson, M. (1937). *Sussex Recipe Book, with a few excursions into Kent*. 1st ed. London: *Country Life*. p.137.

Sinclair, K. (1996). *The Oxford Illustrated History of New Zealand*. 2nd ed. Wellington, New Zealand: Oxford University Press.

Smyth, E. (1919). *Impressions That Remained – Memoirs of Ethel Smyth (2 Vols)*. 1st ed. London: Longmans, Green & Co.

Smyth, E. (1933). *Female Pipings in Eden*. 1st ed. Peter Davies: Edinburgh, pp.208-209.

South Wales Daily News (1873). *South Wales Daily News*. p.2.

Stone, J. (2016). A word about buses ... and fonts! *The Elton Echo*, (46), p.10.

Strachey, R. (1927). *Women's Suffrage and Women's Service.* 1st ed. Westminister. London and National Society for Women's Service.

Strachey, R. (1931). *Millicent Garrett Fawcett.* 1st ed. London: J. Murray, p.60.

Taylor, G. and Taylor B.E.M., M. (2015). *Winds of Change in a Sleepy Sussex Village (Rustington).* 1st ed. Woodstock, Oxfordshire: Writersworld, pp.19-53.

The Derbyshire Times (1878). Rectory of Elton. p.7.

The Framlingham Weekly News (1871). The Enfranchisement of Women. p.4.

The Graphic (1880). A Women's Demonstration. pp.511, 512, 516.

The Ipswich Journal (1869). Bazaar at Aldeburgh. p.8.

The Ipswich Journal (1871). Miss Rhoda Garrett's Lecture on Women's Rights. p.9.

The Ipswich Journal, and Suffolk, Norfolk, Essex and Cambridgeshire Advertiser (1873). Current Topics. p.5.

The Staffordshire Daily Sentinel (1875). From our London Correspondent. p.4.

The Star, Guernsey (1875). Women's Suffrage. p.2.

The Taranaki Daily News (1919). Personal. [online] p.7. Available at: http://paperspast.natlib.govt.nz/newspapers/TDN19190716.2.66 [Accessed 19 Nov. 2016].

The West Sussex Gazette (1936). The Late Mrs Day's Notes on Old Rustington.

UK Parliament. (1866). *Collecting the Signatures for the 1866 Petition.* [online] Available at: https://www.parliament.uk/about/living-heritage/transformingsociety/electionsvoting/womenvote/parliamentary-collections/1866-suffrage-petition/collecting-the-signatures/ [Accessed 8 Feb. 2017].

Wanganui Chronicle (1910). Personal. [online] p.4. Available at: http://paperspast.natlib.govt.nz/newspapers/WC19100121.2.16 [Accessed 18 Nov. 2016].

Wanganui Chronicle (1919). Personal. [online] p.4. Available at: http://paperspast.natlib.govt.nz/newspapers/WC19190204.2.19 [Accessed 19 Nov. 2016].

Western Times (1875). Women's Suffrage. p.3.

Index

PRINTED AND BOUND BY:
Copytech (UK) Limited trading as Printondemand-worldwide,
9 Culley Court, Bakewell Road, Orton Southgate.
Peterborough, PE2 6XD, United Kingdom.